MW00614525

ALSO BY HONORÉE CORDER

You Must Write a Book: Boost Your Brand, Get More Business & Become the Go-To Expert

I Must Write My Book: The Companion Workbook to You Must Write a Book

The Prosperous Writer book series

Prosperity for Writers: A Writer's Guide to Creating Abundance

Prosperity for Writer's Productivity Journal

The Nifty 15: Write Your Book in Just 15 Minutes a Day!

The Prosperous Writer's Guide to Making More Money: Habits, Tactics, and Strategies for Making a Living as a Writer

---

Business Dating: Applying Relationship Rules in Business for Ultimate Success

Tall Order: Organize Your Life and Double Your Success in Half the Time

Vision to Reality: How Short Term Massive Action Equals Long Term Maximum Results

The Divorced Phoenix: Rising from the Ashes of a Broken Marriage

If Divorce is a Game, These are the Rules: 8 Rules for Thriving Before, During and After Divorce

The Successful Single Mom book series

The Miracle Morning book series

ALSO BY BRIAN D. MEEKS (SOMETIMES ARTHUR BYRNE)

Henry Wood Detective series (1-4)

Underwood, Scotch, and Wry

Underwood, Scotch, and Cry

Secret Doors: The Challenge

A Touch to Die For

ARTHUR BYRNE

The Magellan Apocalypse series (1-3)

Killing Hemingway

Beautiful Gears

Published by Honorée Enterprises Publishing

Cover design: Dino Marino ∽ Interior design: 3CsBooks.com

Tradepaper ISBN: 978-1-947665-03-3
Digital ISBN: 978-1-947665-02-6

THE PROSPEROUS WRITER SERIES

THE NIFTY 15

Write Your Book in Just 15 Minutes a Day!

....

HONORÉE CORDER
AUTHOR, *PROSPERITY FOR WRITERS*
& BRIAN D. MEEKS

Published by Honorée Enterprises Publishing

Cover design: Dino Marino ꩜ Interior design: 3CsBooks.com

Tradepaper ISBN: 978-0-9980731-1-8
Digital ISBN: 978-0-9980731-0-1

First edition, October 2016

Special Invitation

Many like-minded individuals have gathered in an online community to share ideas, render support, and promote accountability. When I first wrote *Prosperity for Writers*, I envisioned helping numerous writers shatter the belief that they must starve to survive. I had no idea what was in store, and the result is an amazing community of 700+ writers, authors, editors, and more!

I'd like to personally invite you to join the Prosperity for Writers Mastermind at HonoreeCorder.com/Writers and Facebook.com/Groups/ProsperityforWriters where you will find motivation, daily support, and help with any writing or self-publishing questions.

You can connect with me personally on Twitter @Honoree, or on Facebook.com/Honoree. Thank you so much for your most precious resource, your time. I look forward to connecting and hearing about your book soon!

Table of Contents

INTRODUCTION

We are delighted you're here. We, Brian D. Meeks and Honorée Corder, are prosperous writers, and we want to help you become one too. We're both sharing our points of view in this book, and we'll be sure to let you know who's doing the talking.

Brian writes mostly fiction across five genres under his name and a pen name. He's been at it since January 2, 2010, and he makes his living as an author. Crafting snark with a side order of mockery is one of his very favorite things to do. Honorée writes serious-with-a-side-of-humor nonfiction for business professionals, divorcées, single parents, college-bound students, aaaannnnddd *writers.*

A Few Words from Honorée

Can you really write that novel or nonfiction book in just 15 minutes a day? I say a resounding yes! I've written more than 20 books, and all of them have been written (including this one) between speaking engagements, coaching calls, making breakfast for my daughter, or even during the commercials of my favorite television programs. What I've never had, much to my chagrin, is unlimited time to sit, ponder, and write. As a busy mom, wife, friend, coach, speaker, the owner of multiple businesses ... you get the picture—I've had to squeeze in writing books.

I'm asked this question a lot: *How do you write all those books?* My answers are contained in this quick read, which will get you motivated and inspired to plan and write your book, over the next 100 days, in just 15 minutes a day!

Here's the fun part: I'm writing my sections of this book while Brian simultaneously writes his book *Beautiful Gears* using the formula set forth here. While Brian has many books to his credit, we wanted a real-time, real-world example that in just 15 minutes a day, what we call the "Nifty 15," writing a book is possible.

In addition, he shares "his side of the story," in other words, his thoughts, ideas, and advice for finding time to write and making the most of that time. As you'll see, it's entirely possible! We believe that if it's possible for us, it's possible for you too.

Before we dive in, here are ...

A Few Words from Brian

Writing a book is as much a mindset as it is banging out the words on the keyboard. I couldn't think in terms of writing an entire book until I'd written seven novels and one nonfiction book. Prior to that moment, I couldn't imagine it was possible despite evidence to the contrary.

The voice in my head kept reminding me of the dread I felt when assigned a 1,000-word paper in college. The thought of a novel, which can contain 50,000 words or many more, was so much worse that I just wouldn't consider it.

I could, however, write 1,000 words, and do it in a fairly short time (historically, hours before class after waking from a dead sleep in terror). With this knowledge of my experience, I simply "pantsed" the next 1,000 words of the story without any concern for what came next. I didn't know, and I didn't care.

Now, I've written 11 novels, and my thought process has changed. The voice in my head no longer fights me on writing a new novel. In fact, it encourages me. Typing out 50,000 words is no more daunting than making a bacon, egg, and cheese sandwich for breakfast, though it is, admittedly, less yummy.

So now we embark on an adventure to make the process even easier. I've never tried writing 15 minutes per day. I have written for much longer time periods and done it every day, but I've also known I wasn't using my time effectively. I allowed distractions to get in the way.

The Nifty 15 isn't just about getting from sentence one to *The End.* It's about accomplishing that goal in a way that writing becomes a part of your life that's so routine it's indistinguishable from the other parts of your day. And this routine pays *royalties.*

1

THE PROSPEROUS WRITER'S FORMULA

15 Minutes a Day x 100 Days = Your New Book!

As a busy mom and businessperson, Honorée is constantly on the run and juggling more things than she cares to count on any given day at any given time. We are certain you can relate! We also know what it's like to have a goal in mind and feel the frustration of making slow progress or no progress at all for long periods. If you're like us, you probably have had "write a(nother) book" on your to-do list for a long time. Well, we want to help you change "I'd like to write a book" to "I'm writing my book," which will quickly turn into, "My book is done!" And we don't mean for this project to hang over your head for the next year or two. Nope, we want you to start your book and get it done in four months' time. So we're putting some firm parameters around our suggestions. The framework is simple, straightforward, and the best part, it's gonna work!

If you're like a lot of writers we know, you have been working on writing a book for what seems like forever. We know dozens of now-published authors who say it took them two, three, or even five years or more to finally type "The End" on the final page of their manuscript, call it good, and publish it. (Or delete or shred it, depending upon their personality.) If you fall into this category, don't despair because you're not alone. But we think it's high time you made the decision to just get 'er done and use our guidance and support to do it.

If you're ready, and we hope you are, keep reading!

Why Just 15 Minutes a Day?

In her previous life as an executive coach, Honorée's clients cited lack of time as one of the biggest blocks that got in the way of business development. Her tried-and-true solution is something she calls the "first and *x*." The *X* stands for the number of minutes, ideally between 8 and 15 minutes per day total, her clients committed to working on a business development activity they identified that would move the needle. In most instances, individuals can identify the people they need to develop a relationship with and send an email or make a phone call to set up a meeting in that short amount of time.

Why 15 minutes? Because no one can say, even on their busiest day, "I don't have 15 minutes." (Well, you can, but we're going to call you out on this one.) Finding a block of two to three hours? "Next to impossible," they say. "All my hours are taken." Despite days filled with work product, endless conference calls, and meetings, they can still yield a measly 15 minutes for business development. The same holds true for writers: Even on days when you're committed from before sunup to long after sundown, you can find 15 uninterrupted minutes to write some words. Right?

Right! Especially when you're constantly on the lookout for it and making it a priority. With commitment and planning on your part, you can craft and write your book in just 15 minutes a day over the next 100 days.

Why 100 Days?

We are again borrowing from Honorée's tool kit and using 100 days as the sweet spot of time to make measurable progress on, and accomplish, a defined goal. While you can read all about her 100-day philosophy and process in her book *Vision to Reality*, we'll give you the 30,000-foot overview here. In her experience, 30 days is not enough time to make measurable progress on a goal; it just doesn't allow for true movement and momentum. You're barely getting started and bam! Time's up! At the other end of the spectrum. if you have an entire year to accomplish something, well, that allows for procrastination because there's simply not enough urgency.

One hundred days provides a tight period of time and creates sufficient urgency while simultaneously allowing enough time for you to complete at least the first draft (and we would submit you can write, edit, and publish your manuscript in that period of time, if you put your mind to it).

We suggest you do two things as an aspiring author: Choose to develop a 15-minute daily writing *habit* and give yourself a 100-day deadline.

These two choices will dramatically increase the chances, if not ensure, you will reach the goal of producing your book. Isn't that exciting!? We think *yes.*

You might be wondering how we think you'll be able to do all this writing in such a short period. Well, let us break it down to simple math:

The average typist, according to The Google, types about 40 words per minute (on the low end) and 100 WPM on the high end (Honorée types about 140 WPM, and Brian types about 60 WPM if being tested, but slower when writing). The numbers reveal that, in only 15 minutes at 40 WPM, a writer can accumulate 600 words per day. Over the course of 100 days, an astounding 60,000 words would be written.

Because you probably type just about everything, from email to letters, papers to reports, and even proposals, and especially because you're a writer, your speed is more likely closer to 100 WPM. If that's the case, you could conceivably crank out 1,500 words for every 15 minutes of writing (if you're typing), for a total of 150,000 words over the course of 100 days. And guess what? Those 150,000 words are the equivalent of not just one but *three* full-length novels!

If you're using dictation to crank out the words, you can multiply your output by two, three, or even more. Chris Fox, the author of *5,000 Words Per Hour,* shares some of his encouraging thoughts on dictation. "Dictation is a wonderful tool in my writing arsenal. I can use it in places where writing is inconvenient, like when hiking. The best part? I tend to average about 1,400 words in fifteen minutes. That means in one quick sprint I can crank out an entire chapter, and if I do more than one I can quickly hit that coveted 5,000 words per hour."

Rachel Aaron's *2K to 10K: Writing Faster, Writing Better, and Writing More of What You Love* is a sound reference for you as well. Rachel shares not only how to write faster, she also dives into how to actually write. A total bonus: She shares how to make writing fun, faster, and easier.

Between these two quick-read books, you'll find simple and advanced writing hacks that will help you make the most of your 15 minutes each and every time you sit down to write. Don't worry, we won't leave you hanging. If you purchased this book to find out how to crank out more words, we've added some cool tricks of our own.

As a matter of fact, both of us are big believers in the power of a proven concept. So as we mentioned earlier, Brian is writing a brand new novel while writing this book. He's going from concept to finished manuscript within the 100 days we've decided to write *The Prosperous Writer's Nifty 15*. Keep an eye out for his interjections about his progress, and you can read his full account at the end of this book!

Can It Really Be That Easy?

Now we know what you're probably thinking, that you're not just going to sit down and start writing and the words are going to flow each and every time in just that amount. And you would be right! However, with some prudent preparation and planning (say that three times fast), you will be able to write during your 100 days, if not an entire book, the really solid beginnings of one.

What we're suggesting, that you have the opportunity and ability to write a book in 100 days by writing just 15 minutes a day, is simple but not easy. Even with a positive attitude, a rock-solid plan, and a bucket full of intention, it probably won't be *easy* for you. There will be days when you are busy from the minute you wake up until your head hits the pillow again. You'll have days when you're not feeling so great, or your kids won't be feeling so great, or some other external factor will bum you out or make you mad. It might even seem as though the moment you decide to finally get this project done, unknown conspirators will seemingly work against you. If you're a fiction writer, you might truly believe in unknown conspirators, but there aren't, we promise

Just as Honorée sat down to write this, one of her favorite clients called unexpectedly. Although she had set her timer for 15 minutes, those 15 minutes were not spent writing this book but instead handling a relatively urgent matter. It took her a total of 40 minutes to get her butt back in the chair and start writing again. Which brings us to the next part of our discussion—we want you to make progress, not expect perfection. Let's talk some more about that, shall we?

Progress, Not Perfection

The goal of writing a book, fiction or nonfiction, well, it's a biggie. And like anything worth pursuing, you need to make measurable progress toward the goal consistently. As we mentioned earlier, you can expect delays, denials, and some ugly roadblocks. What you do with challenges, however, is up to you.

We suggest you commit to writing 15 minutes a day for 100 days straight. The more days in a row you go, the more you will enjoy the power of momentum. But what happens when you come down with the flu, your computer crashes, or an unexpected work project pops up? Let's first discuss what not to do: You don't give up. Here's some simple advice we think will help. Don't let one missed day turn into two missed days. If you miss one day, you've missed only 15 minutes. We submit that you'll be able to write for thirty minutes the next day, and no one will be the wiser, right? By all means, make up the time if you can, but under no circumstances are you to let two days turn into three or three days turn into five or five days turn into seven, okay?

The only time we think it's okay for you to miss more than two days in a row is if you are saving women and children in a war-torn country or have gotten lost in the woods and trapped under something heavy. Even then, we will need you to text us a picture of your predicament or at least post it on Instagram as proof. In all seriousness, we want you to focus on making progress on your manuscript every day. If you miss a day here and there, do your best to make up the time, recommit to your goal, and keep going.

A true exception to this rule is a special event or vacation. There is real evidence that taking breaks, vacations, and sabbaticals provide incalculable benefits. While Honorée generally works in 100-day sprints, during almost every sprint is a vacation of some sort (usually a week but sometimes two), a conference, or even a mastermind meeting. Those breaks allow for resting and recharging or learning and networking—all of which provide a boost to her overall productivity in the long run.

Your Personal Rule

One other helpful thing you can do is define a personal rule you never break, no matter what. Personal rules are decisions made in advance about some aspect of life, and we're sure you already have some in place. Some examples include: I don't eat red meat, I don't drink my calories, I always exercise in the morning, or I always take the interstate instead of side streets. People often develop these personal rules by accident, but we suggest you be deliberate in identifying a personal writing rule and then refuse to break that sucker, *no matter what.*

Honorée's personal rule is that she never takes off two days in a row unless it's during one of her two-week family vacations. Here are her thoughts on this topic:

To keep my writing muscles strong, I write something every day. I'm usually working on at least three projects at a time: the one I'm planning, the one I'm writing, and the one I'm publishing. In addition, I have several blogs I write. So, there's always something that needs my attention and that actually helps me to be productive every day … I may not be in the mood to write on a particular project, but I can crank out words on at least one thing!

Having the right tool can help maintain your personal rule. I used to use the web-based Egg Timer (http://e.ggtimer.com/15minutes) but recently adopted Chris Fox's 5,000 WPH App on my iPhone. Not only does it sound an alarm and provide a visual countdown I can see at a glance, it also allows me to record my daily word counts (and share on social media when I'm feeling brave). I like the accountability and tracking combination. In the best possible way, I'm competing against myself. I do not want to break my streak! Although I write in the morning most days, if I haven't gotten some words in, even if it's past my bedtime, I will make myself do it. And I'm always so glad I did. Knowing that the app won't log words if I don't write them bugs me.

Brian's rule is that he's awesome at all times … actually, here's what he really had to say:

My rule is to pay attention to how my environment affects my writing. It seems like a simple thing, but this awareness has taught me some valuable lessons about productivity. I used to write in public at coffee shops, diners, or bars on occasion. One day I looked at my word counts, and I noticed that the totals on days I wrote in public were higher than when I wrote at home where there was no possibility for distractions. I could turn off Facebook, my phone, and everything else, and I still didn't produce as much. I achieved an added level of focus by having to tune out the noise, and that let me zero in on the story and get the words down. More on this later.

Just imagine the sort of things you might learn by paying attention. Maybe you like morning writing more than in the afternoon or evening. Perhaps you do better with coffee or tea. It could be that absolute silence makes you sleepy and less productive, but it's hard to guess. If you pay attention to what's going on around you when you write (and track your daily word count), I'm sure you can find the ultimate environment for maximum productivity.

There can, and should be, in our humble opinions, an element of fun to your personal rules. It bugs Honorée, in a good way, when she might break a rule. Paying attention to his surroundings is a positive focus for Brian. We suggest you incorporate fun in your rules, but of course, we don't want you to think we've lost our minds and are only having fun (well, mostly we are), there is a serious side to your rules. They are *rules*, after all, right? Like all rules, there should be consequences when you break them. Honorée's consequence for missing more than two days, on the rare occasion it happens, is twofold: She has to make up the time, and she can't have cream and sugar in her coffee.

Here's Brian sharing a few words about his consequences:

Everyone is different, but I know myself, and the scariest consequence for missing a day is the loss of motivation.

When I'm on a roll with a project, be it writing, exercising, or just trying to lose weight, I know that the voice in my head gets excited about keeping track of my consecutive days. Each time it goes up by one, the little guy gives a chirp of glee.

So, when I've been successful with a habit, like blogging every day, just the thought of disappointing that cheerful part of me is enough to get me over the hump. (Note: I blogged every day for over six years until March 26th of 2016. Now, I barely ever post anymore.) Keep the streak alive as best you can, and if something catastrophic happens, then start a new one.

One Other Important Note

While Honorée covered the importance of mindset in *Prosperity for Writers,* we would be remiss if we didn't mention it here. The single most important factor in your success as a writer are the beliefs you hold about writing. If you don't believe you can write a book, or at least make measurable progress toward one over the course of 100 days, then you won't. No amount of strategy, planning, or intention can override a deeply held belief that something you want isn't possible.

Before you proceed further, we advise you to adopt the belief that, the minute you sit down to write, the words flow from your fingertips easily and effortlessly. As a matter fact, during the time between writing sessions, your more words are dammed up and can't wait to come out. As a result of her beliefs, Honorée always says she doesn't have a writing problem; she has a *finding time to write* problem.

It's a funny thing about the words we speak out loud, the thoughts we hold in our minds, and the beliefs we hold in our hearts. Those words, thoughts, and beliefs are excellent predictors of our realities. So if on the off chance you have bought into any commonly held negative belief, such as writer's block might be a real thing, or if you write something it's not going to sell, or that the Kindle gold rush is over, you might as well give up. It's in your best interest to recognize that those thoughts, words, and beliefs don't serve you. Further, you would be wise to adopt some new beliefs that may seem crazy, outlandish, or perhaps downright impossible at first. Begin affirming "every time I sit down to write the words flow from my fingertips!" It may not happen the first, fifth, or even the tenth time you sit down to write. But we promise, if you keep at it, the time will come when you'll need to learn to either type or talk faster because the words will always be right there waiting to be born.

If you think something like writer's block is not just a belief but a given, we suggest you listen to almost any episode of *The Writer Files* podcast with Kelton Reid.

He asks his guests, "Do you believe in writer's block?" Almost all of them say "No!" His guests aren't slouches: they are award-winning, full-time, prosperous writers in every niche and genre that exists. Think award-winning journalist Adam Skolnick, Oscar nominated screenwriter Emma Donoghue (of *Room* fame), best-selling author Jeff Goins, and Fast Company editor Joe Berkowitz, among many amazing others.

Remember, these successful writers are not special. They've just owned their greatness a bit sooner than the rest of us. We suspect they got there because they stopped believing in anything that didn't help them get where they wanted to go. And they engaged in a discipline much like the one we're suggesting here: daily writing. All successful, prosperous writers have, among other things, this in common: They treat their writing like a job. They do it when they feel like it *and* when they don't.

It's a widely accepted fact that, on days when the words are harder to come by, you'll oftentimes read those "tough" words later and discover they are pretty awesome. If they aren't, it is true that the more you write, the better you write. Remember that even a rough first draft can be shaped and polished into something wonderful.

Not unlike every other positive habit you strive to develop, a daily writing habit will seem like an excellent idea ... at first. You can't wait to write! You set the timer! You write, and the 15 minutes seem to fly by. You're excited about tomorrow! But after several days, the shiny newness of writing daily wears off (think about all the New Year's resolutions to hit the gym, lose 25 pounds, and take an "after photo"). Our enthusiasm, like our willpower, has a shelf life. That's why developing the daily habit of writing will serve you at the highest level over the long run. You brush your teeth not because you feel like it, but because it's a habit.

Writing will take on the same level of importance (and ease) to you, especially when you diligently track your progress in income and word count. Implementing the Nifty 15 will help you to continue your quest for completing your book long after the initial enthusiasm is gone.

Treating your writing like a job may sound like we're saying it's akin to a job. Yup, that's right, your writing is, or can be, your job. Keep in mind, it's a job you choose based on doing something you already love. You can't *not* write, right? But there are aspects of every job in every career, that aren't fun, sexy, or exciting, *all the time*. You won't like every minute of it, but what's the alternative? Your options include staying at your day job, finding another one, or abandoning your writing career altogether. That is not something that either of us would consider. So, come rain or shine, good health or sinus infection, new *House of Cards* season ready for binging or not, we write.

Here are two mantras that help us stay on track:

1. Do something today that *your future self* will thank you for!
2. Don't give up what you *want* for what you want *right now*.

We want you to get as much as you can from *The Prosperous Writer's Nifty 15*, so we've provided exercises to help you get to work and apply the knowledge we share in each chapter. You'll find them at the end of each chapter, and we've collected them at the end of the book, so that you'll have them all in one place as well.

We've got some more tips and strategies to help you keep your fingers moving and the words coming. But first, do your exercises from this chapter (and don't worry … we've compiled them all at the end of the book for easy reference).

Chapter I Exercises

1. Commit to writing 15 minutes a day over the course of 100 days. Identify your day one (and then ask Siri what the date is 100 days from then). Example: If day one is February 16, day 100 is May 26 (in a leap year).
2. Identify your work in progress (WIP). Remember it's a work in *progress*, not a work in *perfection*. Your goal is to make progress daily over the course of 100 days.
3. Adopt the belief that you write whenever you sit down to do so. Reinforce that, and any other positive belief you need, by reading other encouraging books, listening to podcasts that share the stories of other successful writers, and joining a community of like-minded writers (we suggest the Prosperity for Writers Mastermind on Facebook).
4. Write these two sayings on 3X5 cards and post them where you'll see them when you need them the most:

    - Do something today your *future self* will thank you for!
    - Don't give up what you *want* for what you *want right now*!

Once you've done these exercises, you still have plenty to do! So when you're ready, turn the page!

2

PREPARATION AND PLANNING

Brian will tell you that his book *The Magellan Apocalypse: Map Runners* was preceded by some pretty awesome planning. While he fancies himself more of a pantser than a plotter, for this particular project, he took the time to define the characters, outline the plot, and write the story beats. Before this experiment, it used to take him two months to two years to crank out a book. He completed *The*

Magellan Apocalypse in only two weeks! He credits the advanced planning he did for the incredible speed with which he was able to write this book.

Honorée has written almost two dozen nonfiction books and is currently planning her first novel. Her process includes an outline with potential chapter titles and topics at first. The next step is to flesh out each of the topics and then expand them into subtopics. This process enables her to write books quickly. In fact, she wrote a 65,000-word nonfiction book in the summer of 2015 in only eight days.

You can find several fantastic books on how to do prewriting and book planning. We recommend *Take Off Your Pants* by Libbie Hawker and *The Snowflake Method* by Randy Ingermanson. Brian learned beat writing from *How to Plan and Outline Novels (Using Scrivener)* by Sean Platt under the moniker The Smarter Artist. For nonfiction authors, we humbly suggest Honorée's *You Must Write a Book: Boost Your Brand, Get More Business, and Become the Go-To Expert.*

What we know for sure is this: To make the most of your 15 minutes every day, you need to be prepared. Knowing what you're going to write before you sit down to write is your best bet. We understand that sometimes characters take you down an unanticipated dark alley, or that in the middle of a self-help book you might realize you need to add an entirely new section. But spending at least a couple days getting organized, gathering your thoughts, and jotting down the general direction of the book and chapters is going to help you rock the words.

Now, here are a few steps to get you moving in the right direction.

1. Set your dates.

At the end of the last chapter, we told you to decide on the dates for your 100 days. Having a hard start and stop in mind will do wonders for engineering your success. Do yourself a favor and set a pretty short runway to get started. You don't need weeks to think this through. Pick a date in the next five to ten days and get going! Decide when your day one is going to be, and circle it on your calendar. Then define your 100th day and circle it on your calendar. Every day, you'll know the day you're on, and that should apply subtle pressure to keep your daily habit.

2. Define your project.

Prior to your day one, decide on your genre, main characters, and plot. Or, in the case of nonfiction, determine the main takeaway for your readers. In either case, prepare the most detailed outline possible.

3. Schedule your Nifty 15.

For at least the first 10 days, schedule your 15 minutes each day. If you use a digital calendar, schedule your 15-minute writing block and include a reminder in case you're busy doing something else when the time comes. If you use a paper calendar, you better put those suckers in ink! Unless you have a bona fide emergency, like major blood loss or a fire, do everything possible to write on schedule.

4. Enroll your people.

If you're single, like Brian, and already a full-time writer, good for you. You can write whatever the heck you want, whenever you want, and that's amazing! The rest of us chickens need a different plan. Most likely you have a spouse, kids, a job or two, and even some friends who like to see you on occasion. Assuming that all these people are incredibly supportive of your goals and dreams, you'll want to enroll them in this process. By enroll, we mean tell them what you're doing, ask for their help, and if they were to hold you accountable by asking how you're doing on occasion, that would be great too.

5. Get to writing, Sparky!

It's time for the rubber to meet the road, and for you to get to writing. Honorée has a recurring appointment to write every morning at 6:00 a.m. These words were written just after that hour, as a matter of fact. She schedules a daily appointment on her digital calendar, and it reminds her every day at 5:50 that she's got 10 minutes to get ready to write. Brian's schedule varies from day-to-day, but he defines when he's going to write on any given day ahead of time, and then he does it. So can you!

Chapter 2 Exercises

1. Do the necessary planning and preparation, including reading the books we've suggested or taking a course. We know you're anxious to get started (we completely get it), *and* we know proper preparation helps massively increase productivity and saves a ton of time.
2. Enroll your people and get their support.
3. Start writing! (Yay!)

Are you ready to continue? Alrighty then, turn the page.

3

WRITING THE WORDS

We've talked, at least in general terms, about the reality that you can write lots and lots of words in very small chunks of time. But if you're like us, sometimes it feels as if the very first words are the scariest.

We want to get the ink flowing or cursor moving for you right away, if possible, and we thought it would be helpful to dive a little deeper into the specifics of getting the words out of your head and on paper. We're going to cover three important components: the *how*, the *when*, and the *where*. With fierce determination and the mastery of these three components, before you know it, you'll be off to the races and cranking out content like nobody's business.

The How

How to capture your words is an important decision. The way we see it, you've got options. You can handwrite (longhand or shorthand), type, or dictate your words. Both of us use a combination of all three because sometimes it's easy to jot down a few words on a napkin, other times typing is the wisest play, and in the right circumstances (and with a pretty badass setup), dictation is the fastest and best way to go. Why, you ask? We're going to dive into each one, so you'll know.

Writing by Hand

While it is unlikely you'll reach top speed this way, you can handwrite your manuscripts. It's not our preferred method, but on the rare occasion when technology fails or is inaccessible, good, old-fashioned paper and pencil can do quite nicely, thank you very much. Again, this is the slowest, and in our humble opinions possibly the most painful way to write (writer's cramp, anyone?), but it might be what works best for you. There are times when using a laptop or even your phone to record words would appear rude (at church, a staff meeting, or while watching TV with your family), but whip out a journal or notepad, and almost no one will question your notetaking. Honorée always has her Bullet Journal on hand and has been known to find inspiration in lots of different places (which shall remain undisclosed at this time, but you can certainly ask if you'd like).

Brian had this to share:

The second best thing about the dream of being a full-time author is carving out time to work on that first, second, or even third book. When I began, I was writing one chapter a few times per week on my "blahg" (yes, that's how I spell it).

I had a full-time job on the phones taking orders for J. Crew. During the Christmas season, it was super busy, but the rest of the year there might be periods of five or ten minutes between calls. I kept a notepad nearby, and with my trusty mechanical pencil added to my WIP. Often it was only a sentence or two, but when it was time for my lunch break, I'd get right back at it.

Each night I'd take the handwritten bits and type them into my main WordPress file. It wasn't an efficient way to write, but it allowed me to feed my passion even when I was doing a job that was slowly sucking the life out of me. Every word counts!

Quite possibly, the most famous author of the modern age who writes by hand is J. K. Rowling. Sitting in warm coffee shops as a single mum while her daughter slept, she wrote out the original *Harry Potter* books by hand. Handwriting anything takes longer and leaves little option for easy editing, and yet if that's the way you're going to get your manuscript written, then by all means, it's a fine choice. Embrace it!

Unless you were educated in the 50s, 60s, or 70s, you probably didn't learn shorthand. But if you are a lady or a gentleman of a certain age, shorthand could be a fun and quick option. Total bonus: the people around you will never, *ever*, have any idea what you've written!

Even if you don't handwrite your first draft, you may find, that printing out the full first draft and editing it by hand works well. Honorée has used that effectively for most of her manuscripts, but also keeps her computer handy for making more substantive edits and additions on the fly.

Typing

The lion's share of writers type their words. Whether using an old-fashioned manual, a Selectric with built in Auto Correct, or the latest MacBook Air or iPad Pro, typing is currently the dominant and also an incredibly effective choice for writing. Once one has mastered the skill of typing, the only thing standing between them and their finished manuscript is the time to get 'er done.

Mat Morris, the host of the *Author Strong Podcast*, has a nifty little gadget with no screen. Hence, he can perform no real-time editing, just typing, typing, typing. What's interesting is that he sometimes can write 50,000 words in one day. Honorée uses her Mac and iPad. Brian uses an iPad with a blue tooth keyboard and the Storyist app. Between the two of us, we have managed to write sometimes thousands of words per day on a consistent basis over the course of several years.

Dictation

Another option is dictation. Dictation has been around for a long time, but dictating fiction and nonfiction alike has reached new levels of popularity recently. Authors craft their main titles via dictation, but also talk and write books about it (see the aforementioned books by Chris Fox and Rachel Aaron). Honorée tried two earlier versions of Dragon Dictate (and slayed the dragon both times) before the most recent version was released. This time she was able to train her Dragon and now dictates just about everything. While her typing speed is nothing to sneeze at, she can dictate at double or triple that speed in some instances. On several occasions, she has topped 2500 words in a Nifty 15 sprint. Brian has tried Dragon Dictate as well, but after considerable effort with both the computer and mobile versions, was found dead along the side of the dictation highway. It isn't for everyone.

If you're going to give it a go, you'll want to make sure you have the proper equipment. Honorée recently started using Dragon Anywhere, which is the iPhone app version of Dragon Dictate. For that version to work most effectively, she needed to purchase an extra set of headphones (which also work for dictating into Google Doc on her iPad) to keep in her purse for recording on the go. She keeps a pair for dictating into her MacBook Air as well. Brian still doesn't like it one bit, and is still bitter about the whole death thing mentioned above.

Our point is you have to be intentional and strategic about the resources and tools you'll need to be effective and efficient during your daily Nifty 15 writing sprints and have them available when and where you need them.

Regardless of how you choose to write, your preferences and style might change over time, as they have for us. That said, we recommend you make a choice and master it before trying others.

The When

Two other questions you might have rolling around in your mind: *When do I fit in my fifteen minutes? What's the best time?* In the spirit of all those recovering lawyers-turned-novelists out there, we give you our answer: it depends. Are you working the graveyard shift? A stay-at-home mom of six children? A sales rep who works six and seven days a week, 12–14 hours a day? You'll notice we didn't ask if you were an unemployed, independently wealthy thirty-something because that's just about the only category of person who has an unlimited amount of time to write. The rest of us have to fit it in, at least until we've graduated to full-time, prosperous writer.

It's worth noting again that no one can say, no matter how busy they are, that they don't have 15 minutes at some point during the day to write. And by no one, we mean *you.* The question then becomes *when are those 15 minutes?* It will depend on your regular schedule, other commitments you have, and when you tend to write best.

Let's address the last thoughts first. Honorée is a morning person and is convinced her best writing happens in the morning. Brian is a night owl and tends to do his best writing just about any time after lunch. Both of us know that when we have the time to write the words, the words can and must be written. We don't have the luxury of embracing a belief that limits our abilities, and we don't think you do either. It will serve you to adopt the belief, as we mentioned earlier, that when you sit down to write, the words flow freely, easily, and effortlessly from your fingertips. We both have our preferred times of the day to write, but when it comes down to it, we write when it is on our schedule to write. No excuses, just words. Lots and lots of words.

Which leaves us with your regular schedule and other commitments. If you have a standard 9-to-5 job, you have several options available. You could wake up 15 minutes earlier than normal and roll out of your bed and on to the computer. If you take public transportation, you could write on the bus or train. Mark Dawson, the author of the John Milton series, was a full-time lawyer who wrote during his commute to and from London every day for years (and now he's a full-time prosperous author because of his consistency and dedication).

You're probably going to have to get creative if up to this point you've been at a loss for when you might fit in some writing. Work permitting, you could arrive 15 minutes early and write before work begins. You could write during a 15-minute break or during your lunch hour. Stay after work and write in the break room, an empty office, or conference room. If you don't have to rush home after work to make dinner for your family, or even if you do, what's the harm in stopping at a Starbucks on the way, for only 15 minutes, and cranking out a chapter? If all else fails, take your computer to bed with you, set your timer for 15 minutes, and write before you call it a day. Honorée has been known to employ every single one of those tactics, sometimes all in one day, especially when she's on a deadline.

We think it's a great idea for you to analyze your schedule and decide well in advance when your 15 minutes is going to be every day. Then add writing to your schedule just as you would a doctor's appointment or some other nonnegotiable block of time. If you're pretty sure you can write at the same time every day, make the appointment recurring. If you're going to write at different times on different days, then manually write in or electronically schedule your writing time on your calendar. Be sure to set an alert for 5, 10, or 15 minutes in advance to remind you writing time is coming right up.

Honestly, the best time to write is when you have time to do so. Actually, it's when you make the time to write. No one ever has time to sit down and write any more than they have time to get an additional college degree or train for a marathon.

Something we both know for sure is this: If writing and your writing business is important enough to you, you will do whatever it takes to write.

The Where

Our next subtopic on getting the words out is where you can write. This one is simple: We believe you can write anywhere you find yourself. You can dictate words into your phone while you get ready in the morning. Or while you're on the treadmill, doing dishes, or taking an afternoon walk. You can write at a coffee shop, in the passenger seat of a moving car, on an airplane, and in a hotel room (or hotel lobby). You can write anywhere, especially with the right belief around words flowing anytime an opportunity presents itself.

Why are we being so adamant in making this point? Because we have heard of people who believe they can't write unless they are facing east at sunset on a Tuesday with a fresh cup of coffee (with half-and-half and two Splenda). Along with believing that words come easily to you, you've also got to believe the words will flow whenever and wherever you are. Let's face it, even when you are a full-time writer, perfect conditions rarely present themselves. You have to believe all conditions are permanently perfect and, as such, are perfect for you to write the words.

Brian's best "where" is in a crowded bar, café, or restaurant as he mentioned earlier. He doesn't just prefer those public venues; he's found that his productivity increases by a fair margin, backed by data, as he will tell you.

I love data, and for a while, I tracked my daily word count. I would add each entry to an Excel spreadsheet with the date before I went to bed.

One day I decided to add a new column for location, home or public, and another for length of work session. The long and short of it is that the data showed that my productivity increased by about 20 percent when I was forced to tune out the noise of a public environment.

I've since read an article that explains the why of it all, and it turns out there is some science behind being creative in public. In a study published in the *Journal of Consumer Research* (Vol. 30, No. 4), Ravi Mehta, Rui (Juliet) Zhu, and Amar Cheema concluded that moderate ambient noise creates a distraction that helps people think imaginatively. They found that "walking out of one's comfort zone and getting into a relatively noisy environment may trigger the brain to think abstractly, and thus generate creative ideas."

My point is simply that you may want to try different places and keep a notebook or Excel sheet with your results. You may learn something valuable.

Say No

One very effective strategy you can employ immediately (and forever) to help your daily writing habit is saying no. In fact, *no* can and should be your first response when anyone asks you to do anything. Just imagine how much extra time you'll have when you say no to the things you really don't want to do anyway. Here are a few items you'll want to avoid: meetings with no purpose, wasting time on social media, and mindlessly watching television. Of course, we love meetings with purpose, enjoy some time on social media, and watch delicious television. But we both learn to say no to the things that are not as important as our writing—until it's done for the day. We hope you do too.

Oh, Yes, the Why

About the only thing we haven't covered so far is your *why*. As part of doing your 100-day plan, you'll see a section called purpose. While your vision is your *what* (as in, what do you want), your purpose is your *why*: Why are you determined to write this book in the first place? What's in it for you? A strong why, combined with a strong positive belief it's possible, will act as writing rocket fuel. You could spend your fifteen minutes each day doing one million other things, right? Yet you've chosen writing a book because, for whatever reason, you have a strong desire to do so, which we completely understand. What we want you to get very clear on is your specific why. Knowing your why is so important because it will carry you through, just like your writing habit, when the going gets tough.

When you know your why, you will say no to opportunities to procrastinate or delay your writing. You'll say yes to yourself and the goal of writing your book when you understand why you want to write it in the first place. Is it to replace the income you make from your job? Create another stream of residual income? Fulfill a lifelong dream of becoming an author? Your why doesn't matter. In other words, there is no wrong why. It just needs to be really strong. Like twenty strands of dental floss strong. Like super glue strong. Because when you declare you're going to do something, obstacles show up to test your true resolve (the aforementioned unseen forces), and we want you to be ready.

So take a few minutes and write down your why.

- Because I can finally be a full-time writer.
- Because I can replace the income from my job.
- Because I've always wanted to be a full-time writer, and I deserve to be one!
- Because I must spend more time with my kids before they are all grown and gone.
- *Because writing is what I was put on this Earth to do, and by golly, I'm going to do it!*

Here Honorée will share a little about her purpose:

I'm very clear on my *why*: I create multiple streams of leveraged income that allow me to spend lots of time with my family. It's important to me that every aspect of the work I do is helpful in some way, contributes to the lives of others, and makes their way in life easier, better, more effective, more efficient, more productive, and more prosperous. So when I discovered the power of writing books and how they allowed me to reach people I might not otherwise meet, and help them, I was in! Writing provides an opportunity almost like no other to add value, inspiration, and set the stage for transformation.

In *Prosperity for Writers,* I encouraged my readers to "BOLO" (be on the lookout) for all the people who were making a prosperous living from their writing, all the ways they could make money from their writing, and basically anything else that reinforced the idea that they, too, could be prosperous, full-time writers. I now get countless messages, tweets, and emails from writers throughout the world telling me how they started to BOLO and then eventually became full-time writers. My why is so simple: to impact as many people as I can in a positive way and encourage them when they might otherwise have no support. The by-product of my why working successfully is that I get to spend lots of time having a blast with my family.

Here is Brian's why: It may sound like sacrilege, but when I decided to turn my focus to writing and cut back my hours at work, my why was *to make money*.

Everyone needs a source of income, and I've always liked the adage "Choose a job you love, and you'll never work a day in your life." I enjoy writing. In fact, I enjoy all aspects of the book business, even the stuff I don't like. Yes, the stuff that I consider to be "dreadful" is only that way because there are other things I prefer to do. Creating print editions is a chore that annoys me, but if I had a job, and in my free time I created print editions of books, well, I'd like it. (Note: This year I'll be hiring someone to do this chore for me along with certain other tasks.) The only reason I dread getting that job done is that I'd rather be writing.

So, my why was clear: "Brian, you're writing because it's the most fun way you can think of to make a living. You're in it for the money."

If the quality of my writing garnered bad reviews, people didn't enjoy reading it, and I couldn't sell my work, well, I wouldn't do it. I would probably pursue woodworking. I enjoy the tales I craft, and since other people do too, it's a reasonable use of my time, and it makes sense that I chose this path for my livelihood. That is my why.

It is so important for you to be clear about your why because, while having a vision (your what) is great, when you know your purpose, you are much more likely to follow through on the what. You're much more likely to *find the time to write your words*, even when it is inconvenient, you're busy trying to accomplish lots of other things, or a good old-fashioned roadblock pops up.

There will be countless opportunities for you not to write. You'll be sick, or someone you love will be sick. You'll have a deadline at work, your tax return will be due, or you'll have figured out you need to register your car or pay a huge fine. When you're clear on your why, you'll make sure you set your alarm 30 minutes earlier on deadline day. You'll turn off the next episode of *Game of Thrones* or put down that thriller you're dying to finish to work on your own story because you know the only way for you to reach your goal of becoming a prosperous writer is to actually write! Without a strong why, it will be much easier for you to "mean to get to writing," or to "get it done tomorrow." The problem is there are seven days in a week, and tomorrow isn't one of them. You won't do it tomorrow if you've been meaning to do it tomorrow for weeks, months, or even years. Even within the structure of the 100 days, without a strong why, you might be tempted to take a few days off here and there or even abandon the process altogether once the newness wears off. We know how great being an author can be, and we both passionately love the book business, so we don't want that to happen to you! We shiver at the thought that you would abandon your quest before you reach success.

We encourage you to draw a line in the sand, state your why, and commit to yourself and your writing like you never have before. Add a recurring appointment in your calendar specifically for writing. An unbreakable appointment that you will move heaven and Earth to show up for, that you declare to your loved ones is really important to you, and one you want their support for. One you don't miss no matter the circumstances.

We know you can do it *because we do it.* We know lots of other people who do it too. They write every single day—rain, snow, shine, or Christmas. Come on, it's only fifteen minutes. Fifteen minutes a day to do something you've wanted to do since you were eight years old: be a writer. But not just any writer, a prosperous full-time writer. The writer who's known, the writer who's admired, talked about, and that supports themselves, their family, and their plans for fun.

Just this last weekend, Honorée's royalties allowed her to take her family to a five-star hotel for the weekend. They ate and shopped. They ordered room service. Went sight-seeing. It was marvelous. And you know what? All three mornings while her family was still sleeping, she got up and wrote for 15–20 minutes (some of the words you're reading right now, in fact), because although she was "on vacation," writing is neither hard, nor an obligation, and it never really feels like a job. She considers herself blessed to be able to write for a living. So she puts in the time, day in and day out. Not because she must, but because she can. And so can you!

Chapter 3 Exercises:

1. Decide how you're going to write, as in, what is the best way for you to capture your words (handwriting, typing, dictating)?
2. When are you going to write each day? Will it be an appointment at the same time every day, or will you decide each day what time you'll write tomorrow?
3. Where is the best place for you to write? At home? In a coffee shop? On the bus or train? If you're going to a public place, what do you need to have with you?
4. Finally, define your why. Why are you committed to finding time to write each day and finishing your book? A strong why will enable you to overcome most, if not all, of the blocks that will show up.

Once you've completed your homework, keep calm and read on.

4

WHILE YOU'RE WRITING

At this point, we hope you're excited to start writing. But here's one thought that might not have occurred to you: There are lots of other things to do to complete your book.

That's right. Because we want you to become a prosperous writer, there are a lot of other items that need to be completed while you're writing your book. You'll need to find readers, there's no doubt about that. The best book in the world doesn't sell without a rockin' cover. If the book's description falls short, your book will languish in obscurity, which is sad especially after you've put in all the work. You may or may not have heard that great books are not written, they are rewritten and edited and proofread. Finally, in order to sell some books, those books actually have to be for sale. As you can see, you have a short but important list of extra tasks you must do, and we're going to suggest that you work on them before you finish your book.

This is by no means a full list, but it will get you started. We suggest finding a book or two on each of the following topics to use as your study guides because, well, we think you should study every aspect of your writing business as you would for any other career from which you want to earn a full-time living.

Let's break these tasks down for you, one at a time.

Build your email list

There are multiple books on the subject of building your list of readers that hopefully become fans, leave positive reviews, and recommend your book to others. You might want to read *The Prosperous Writer's Mini e-Book of Finding Readers* (coming soon!), *Your First 1000 Copies* by Tim Grahl, or *How to Market a Book* by Joanna Penn. In fact, you might want to read all of them because, though the subject matter is generally the same, each contains within them different gems of wisdom you will find helpful.

Get a Book Description

We use, love, and recommend Bryan Cohen. You might know him as the cohost of the *Sell More Books Show*, and you'll find him at BestPageForward.net. Brian is an excellent copywriter, and he most likely is at least part of the reason you are reading this book. Copywriting is a very special skill, different from writing in general. Unless you are a trained copywriter, you'll want to cough up the two hundred bucks or so to have someone write an awesome description of your book. Trust us when we say the increase in sales will return your investment to you many times over.

Brian's Note: I've learned to write solid ad copy by keeping meticulous records about what works and what doesn't. I hated this task for a long time, and it wasn't until I saw measurable proof of my successful ad copy that I started to believe I could do it. This took years.

Brian's Note 30 Days Later: Please disregard my brag about writing solid ad copy. At the time I wrote that note, I was creating ads that were making me piles of money. My assumption was that I was pretty good at it. I was converting about 1 in 30 clicks.

I hadn't actually read anything on the subject, though.

Since writing then, I've undertaken a course of self-study on the art of writing ad copy. After learning a bunch, I rewrote my descriptions on Amazon.

Because I wanted clean data, I chose to advertise only one book at a time and watch the numbers. The impact was immediate, and now my descriptions tend to convert (either for Kindle Unlimited downloads or sale) at a rate of 1 in 6 to 1 in 14, which is *vastly* better than 1 in 30.

The point is that the data I had before showed I was making a profit from my advertising copy, but it didn't tell me if the ad copy was any good. Only by wondering if I could do better did I set up a study that let me find out how wrong my assumptions about my copywriting skills had been.

The moral of this story is keep and review data!

Get a book cover

Correction: *Get an excellent book cover.* Almost nothing is as tragic as a great book with an awful cover. And we have seen it so many times, it's not even funny. If you are someone who thinks *I'll do it myself, I'll have a friend do it*, or *I don't have the money, so I'll buy the cheapest cover I can get*, do yourself a favor: wait. Wait until you have the money to afford a decent cover. There is no sense putting all of the work into planning, writing, editing, rewriting, describing, and marketing a book that someone will look at and immediately dismiss because it looks like crap.

Nothing stops someone from reading a book faster than a crappy cover. You might have to wait a month or two or get a weekend job to be able to afford it, but you and your book are worth it. You deserve to have a great cover to go with your great effort. Don't you agree? Fail to heed our advice, put a mediocre cover on your book, launch it, and see what happens. Soon you'll rank 2.9 million out of 3 million books on Amazon, your mom and two nice friends who don't have the guts to tell you the truth will write five-star reviews for you, and your book won't sell. Will it be worth it? No.

And if you're in a hurry, what are you in such a hurry for? To fail miserably? We think not! We almost (*almost*) suggest you get a great cover even if the writing in your book is terrible. At least your book will sell, even if people won't finish it. Now we're not being serious about that, but we want to make sure you get our point. You do get our point, right?

LINE UP YOUR EDITOR

Any editor worth their salt will be booked months in advance. The minute your 100 days start, maybe even before you've written your first word, find and within a short period of time line up your editor. We highly recommend Writership, a team led by Leslie Watts. She and her crack team of editors can get your manuscript into fine form, but you'll definitely want to get on their calendar. As of this writing, she is booked about three months in advance, which could be ideal for you as about three months from now, you're going to need an editor (if not a bit sooner). If your goal is to have published your book within 100 days, then you'll need to line up your editor right away (Go ahead and do it now, we'll wait).

Set up your books online (KDP, CreateSpace, etc.)

We assume you're going to self-publish, and it's never too early to do some of the administrative tasks necessary as part of launching your book, up to and including setting them up on the various retail sites. You can enter information, such as the book title, subtitle, author(s), other contributors, description, keywords; upload your book cover; and if you're feeling particularly confident, upload your manuscript in its current state and put your book up for pre-order.

Cautionary note: Failure to upload a final product ten days prior to the official launch of your book on KDP when you've put it up for pre-order will get you one year in the book equivalent of Siberia. So, in effect, feeling confident isn't enough. You must be sure you're going to ship your book on time, no matter what.

If you're not planning to self-publish, you'll want to do the requisite research around finding an agent, creating your pitch, etc. Since neither of us have traditionally published, we don't have advice to share other than to encourage you to seek sound advice elsewhere.

One Last Important Note

You won't always feel like doing any actual writing. There is a reason our goal is to consistently knock out one or two thousand words per day, as opposed to tens of thousands. While this is possible considering that we're full-time writers, and therefore have the time to do it, writing thousands or tens of thousands of words per day isn't particularly practical (at least for us) because we have other things we must do, like to do, and want to do. When you "run out of words" or are feeling like your 15 minutes have been well spent, and you want to diversify your book business building activities, there is still much to be done. Keep this chapter handy for when you're at a loss for what to do.

On the other hand, if you are overwhelmed by the seemingly endless list of tasks that need to be done, we want to point out Parkinson's law, which states (in essence) the amount of time you have to perform a task is the amount of time it'll take you to do it. We know you can write a book in 15 minutes a day, and if all you can do is squeak out another 15 minutes to work on the critical book business tasks, use it for marketing, building your list, or even a few minutes of social media. That's not to say you won't need to carve out a few hours a week to put the fine point on your writing business. You will. But as we've discussed, if it truly is that important to you, you will find the time just as we do and many of the other wonderful full-time writers we know do as well.

CHAPTER 4 EXERCISES

1. Study the book business. Just as you would study to become a lawyer, doctor, or air traffic controller, you'll want to constantly study the book business. We have some great suggestions for you. Check out our recommended books, podcasts, and other resources in the back of this book.
2. Begin to build your list. Even if you don't plan to launch your book for two years, you should have a list of people who want to read it. Sign up with Aweber, Mailchimp, or even Infusionsoft and start sending out a regular newsletter (we both prefer Aweber).
3. Hire someone to craft your book description. You'll use this on all the sites where you sell your book and on the back cover of the print edition.
4. Line up your editors and proofreaders. Give them the date you anticipate sending them the first draft for them to review. This will provide an extra piece of accountability, too! (Added bonus!)
5. Set up your accounts online at Amazon (KDP, CreateSpace, and ACX), Barnes and Noble, Kobo, iBooks, Smashwords, Draft2Digital, etc. There's quite a bit to do, so the sooner you can get to it, the better.

We're certain you get the point: writing your book is just the beginning of everything that needs to happen for you to have a successful book! If you're like us, you're itching to get moving. Well then, read the final chapter quickly, review Brian's experience writing *Beautiful Gears* in 15 minutes a day in 100 days (you can get access to it right here: BrianDMeeks.com/Nifty), and start writing!

5

CALL TO ACTION

We hope by now you can't wait to put this book down and start writing. We know from experience that if you take our advice seriously and do the planning we've suggested, you'll be able to knock out your first book in a relatively short period of time. And here's a big promise: When you've done it once and proven to yourself you can do it, the sky is the limit! There will be no end to the books you'll be able to write!

One last thing to keep in mind: The Nifty 15 and 100 days in and of themselves are arbitrary. They constitute an artificial structure that can and will help you to succeed *if you use it*. You know, of course, that you don't need to write for an entire 15 minutes, nor are you limited to 15 minutes. You can write for five minutes or five hours if you so choose and your schedule accommodates your ambitions. One hundred days, while a simple and round number, is arbitrary and open for your revision at any time. We chose 15 minutes, as you know by now, because almost no one can say, "I just don't have 15 minutes a day to write." We wanted to provide the framework for you to create a daily writing habit that would stick. We know some writers who crank out a book a week, and others who write one or two books a year. Lots of people attempt their first book during the annual NaNoWriMo challenge. Here's what we know for sure: 15 minutes a day over the course of 100 days will provide you with the structure and habit installation you need to write your book.

If for some reason you hate the number 15, or you'd rather write your book in 90 days, by all means, have at it. We only hope that if you're going to argue against any of our recommendations, you're arguing *for* the possibilities for yourself and your writing.

We not only wish for you take our advice to heart and write your book, we want you let us know all about it! Be sure to connect with us in the Prosperity for Writers Mastermind Group on Facebook and listen to the *Write Your Podcast* (starring the two of us) on the Blog Talk Radio.

Now that you have an understanding of how to write your book in only 15 minutes a day, you can go forth to calculate and write!

Resources Section

Other books in The Prosperous Writer Book Series

- *Prosperity for Writers: A Writer's Guide to Creating Abundance*
- *The Prosperity for Writers Productivity Journal: A Writer's Workbook for Creating Abundance*
- *The Prosperous Writer's Mini e-Book of Finding Readers*
- *The Prosperous Writer's Mini Guide to Selecting Keywords for Your Book* (coming early 2017)

Links to our newsletters and other awesome-sauceness

- Brian's rough draft of *Beautiful Gears*: BrianDMeeks.com/Nifty
- Two free Chapters of *Prosperity for Writers:* HonoreeCorder.com/writers

Books for Aspiring Writers

- *You Must Write a Book: Boost Your Brand, Get More Business, and Become the Go-To Expert* by Honorée Corder
- *The Miracle Morning for Writers* by Hal Elrod, Steve Scott & Honorée Corder
- *You are a Writer, So Start Acting Like One* by Jeff Goins

Writing and Self-Publishing Podcasts

- *Wordslinger Podcast*
- *The Author Biz Podcast*
- *The Self-Publishing Formula Podcast*
- *The Self-Publishing Podcast*
- *The Sell More Books Show*
- *The Writer Files*

Book Exercises

Chapter 1 Exercises

1. Commit to writing 15 minutes a day over the course of 100 days. Identify your day one (and then ask Siri what the date is 100 days from then). Example: If day one is February 16, day 100 is May 26 (in a leap year).
2. Identify your work in progress (WIP). Remember it's a work in *progress*, not a work in *perfection*. Your goal is to make progress daily over the course of 100 days.
3. Adopt the belief that you write whenever you sit down to do so. Reinforce that, and any other positive belief you need, by reading other encouraging books, listening to podcasts that share the stories of other successful writers, and joining a community of like-minded writers (we suggest the Prosperity for Writers Mastermind on Facebook).

4. Take these two sayings on 3X5 cards and post them where you'll see them when you need them the most:

    - Do something today your *future self* will thank you for!
    - Don't give up what you *want* for what you *want right now*!

Chapter 2 Exercises

1. Do the necessary planning and preparation, including reading the books we've suggested or taking a course. We know you're anxious to get started (we completely get it), *and* we know proper preparation helps massively increase productivity and saves a ton of time.
2. Enroll your people and get their support.
3. Start writing! (Yay!)

Chapter 3 Exercises

1. Decide how you're going to write, as in, what is the best way for you to capture your words (handwriting, typing, dictating)?
2. When are you going to write each day? Will it be an appointment at the same time every day, or will you decide each day what time you'll write tomorrow?
3. Where is the best place for you to write? At home? In a coffee shop? On the bus or train? If you're going to a public place, what do you need to have with you?
4. Finally, define your why. Why are you committed to finding time to write each day and finishing your book? A strong why will enable you to overcome most, if not all, of the blocks that will show up.

Chapter 4 Exercises

1. Study the book business. Just as you would study to become a lawyer, doctor, or air traffic controller, you'll want to constantly study the book business. We have some great suggestions

for you. Check out our recommended books, podcasts, and other resources in the back of this book.

2. Begin to build your list. Even if you don't plan to launch your book for two years, you should have a list of people who want to read it. Sign up with Aweber, Mailchimp, or even Infusionsoft and start sending out a regular newsletter (we both prefer Aweber).
3. Hire someone to craft your book description. You'll use this on all the sites where you sell your book and on the back cover of the print edition.
4. Line up your editors and proofreaders. Give them the date you anticipate sending them the first draft for them to review. This will provide an extra piece of accountability, too! (Added bonus!)
5. Set up your accounts online at Amazon (KDP, CreateSpace, and ACX), Barnes and Noble, Kobo, iBooks, Smashwords, Draft2Digital, etc. There's quite a bit to do, so the sooner you can get to it, the better.

Quick Favor

We're wondering, did you enjoy this book?

First of all, thank you for reading our book! May we ask a quick favor?

Will you take a moment to leave an honest review for this book on Amazon? Reviews are the BEST way to help others purchase the book.

You can go to the link below and write your thoughts. We appreciate you!

http://tinyurl.com/N15review

THE PROSPEROUS WRITER'S GUIDE TO MAKING MORE MONEY

Habits, Tactics, and Strategies for Making a Living as a Writer

HONORÉE CORDER
BRIAN D. MEEKS
AUTHORS OF *THE NIFTY 15*

Published by Honorée Enterprises Publishing

Cover design: Dino Marino ❧ Interior design: 3CsBooks.com

Tradepaper ISBN: 978-0-9980731-6-3
Digital ISBN: 978-0-9980731-5-6

First edition, February 2017

Special Invitation

Many like-minded individuals have gathered in an online community to share ideas, render support, and promote accountability. When I first wrote *Prosperity for Writers*, I envisioned helping numerous writers shatter the belief that they must starve to survive. I had no idea what was in store, and the result is an amazing community of 700+ writers, authors, editors, and more!

I'd like to personally invite you to join the The Prosperous Writer Mastermind at HonoreeCorder.com/Writers and Facebook.com/groups/ProsperityforWriters where you will find motivation, daily support, and help with any writing or self-publishing questions.

You can connect with me personally on Twitter @Honoree, or on Facebook.com/Honoree. Thank you so much for your most precious resource, your time. I look forward to connecting and hearing about your book soon!

TABLE OF CONTENTS

Introduction

We are delighted you're here. We, Brian D. Meeks and Honorée Corder, are prosperous writers.

Brian writes mostly fiction across five genres, under his name and a pen name (Arthur Byrne). He's been at it since January 2, 2010 and makes his living as an author. He enjoys crafting snark with a side order of mockery. Honorée writes nonfiction for business professionals, divorcees, single parents, college-bound students, and, of course, *writers.*

We loved the idea of sharing our knowledge with you, our fellow-writers, so that you, too, could become a full-time (if you so desire), prosperous writer. We hatched the idea of writing a book, this book, so you could take the same journey we've taken: from aspiring full-time writer to actual full-time writer, only in a fraction of the time it has taken us. Part of getting from here to there is getting comfortable with your numbers. Making more money from your writing means understanding your metrics (such as how many books are being sold, how many page reads you're getting if you're enrolled in KDP). It also means understanding how to use math to know if your business is growing, to know how to make it grow faster and easier, and ultimately, to make more money. Oh, and there's one more thing: what to do with your money once you get it! These aspects of the book business aren't as scary or as complicated as you might think.

A Note from Honorée

I'm on record (multiple times) as "hating math." For much of my business life, I avoided looking closely at my numbers for a very long time because I didn't completely understand them. In fact, whenever someone asked me why I chose to pursue goals and coach my clients in 100-day cycles, my answer has *always* been, *I hate math. I don't like to multiply and divide. I want a simple, easy way to keep track of things in my head.* Although it was clearly not enough, all I did was just keep an eye on the bottom line: How much was I making? Was it more than last month? Last quarter? Last year?

You picked up this book because you want to make more money as a writer, right? But already I'm talking about metrics and math. Is this a book about math? Well, yes and no. You see, to make more money, you should not only know how to get it, but you also have to know where to get it—what the best sources are for you. And, once you get it, you need to know what to do with it. While you might be thinking, *I'm pretty sure I know what to do with money when I get it, Honorée*, you might be wrong. Brian and I are going to share some strategies with you in this book that will knock you back in your seat and cause you to behave differently. Which, in turn, will cause you to make more money. But first things first.

Why would someone who is on record as hating math write a book that is, in part, about math? Well, it's all fine and good that I had an aversion to math, but what I didn't know was that it had cost me money. It wasn't until I started paying attention to my metrics (trends, inclinations, and the general direction of my sales) and understanding the math, that my income improved. When I learned the what and the how, I got excited. I realized a few important things:

Metrics and math aren't that difficult, and when I understood them better, I made more money. Just like anything else that at first (second, and fifth) glance seems overwhelming, math is one of those complex concepts that you can grasp easily, if you take it one piece at a time.

Let me say that again: *With an understanding and correct use of metrics and math, I could earn more money.* And without doing more work! What?! Yup, that's right! When you know where to place the fulcrum, you can work the same or less and earn more.

If you're already comfortable with math and metrics, but you just don't like the current results you see, stay with me for a bit longer. There's a lot in here for you, too.

Just like anything you've mastered that once seemed nearly impossible (driving a stick shift or learning a new language, anyone?) opens doorways to new realms, learning not only to understand your metrics and math but also to master them can help you make more money from your writing than you ever thought possible.

When I met the great and wonderful Brian D. Meeks, I was struck by how much he *loves* math. Every single time I say the word math, his response is, *I just love math.* As someone who believes firmly in the power of words of affirmation, I've started saying *I just love math*, too, because you know what? Math is making me more money, and who doesn't love more money? I know, that's why you're here! Embracing math and coming to love it has helped me release my reluctance and embrace the possibilities.

In the event you're ready to return this book from whence it came, I implore you to hang in here! I'm going to take you on a journey, the journey from unconscious incompetence (not knowing what you don't know) to unconscious competence (knowing what you need to know *like a boss*), with Brian guiding us on our path.

Brian is good at math, and he's going to hold your hand, just as he's held mine, and show you how to take the numbers you have and make them as big as you want them to be. He will show you how to read the numbers, how to see where they are going, and (here's the fun and exciting part) how to make the most of them. The two of us together are going to help you maximize your mindset and your money—both directly and indirectly.

What if you could use and understand the numbers you have in such a way that you could increase the "good" numbers, and adjust the "bad" ones? Brian is going to show you everything you need to know, and within the pages of this book, turn you into a math lover, too.

We suggest reading all the way through this book and then start again at the beginning. Take each concept and idea as it comes, learn it and apply it, then continue. What if you're confused or have questions? You're in luck! Brian loves questions, too. We'll tell you in a later section how you can get answers to your questions.

I'm so excited for you to get started, but first, a few words from Brian!

A Note from Brian

I love data. I love math. I love doing math with data a bunch. I, you see, am the son of a mathematician. Dad loves math, too.

If you're cringing because you don't love math, I understand. It didn't come easily to you when you were young, and people tend to gravitate toward the things they do well. It may be tough for me to win the argument that math is cool, considering you've spent your entire life saying (or thinking) how much you hate math every time it comes up, but I'm going to try.

Consider this: remember back in high school when hormones were raging like an ill-tempered mixed martial arts fighter? If you recall, all the pretty girls and handsome guys gravitated toward the kids in math club. Everyone wanted to be cool like the math kids. The players on the football team and the cheerleaders mostly cried themselves to sleep every Friday night because there weren't enough math geniuses to go around.

What? You don't remember it that way? Huh… maybe that's a bad example.

Well, it doesn't matter. What's important is that you'd like to make more money with your books. Honorée and I are going to teach you how to use math and data to do just that. We're going to help point you in the right directions for where and how you can make more money.

What makes me qualified to write about this subject?

I spent seven and a half years as a data analyst with GEICO where a fifteen-minute call could save you 15% on your car insurance. I was in the marketing department, so it was my job to use data and math to find ways to make more money. Also, I have a degree in Economics, which is a lot of algebra, which I love!

What I don't have is a degree in psychology, though I did read an issue of Psychology Today in 1987, so the next bit is based on my vast knowledge of the human psyche.

I'm convinced after thousands of hours of research (or fifteen minutes of thinking about it...give or take) that most people can do most things, and the only barrier holding them back is fear and an abundance of situation-comedies-on-demand through sites like Hulu, Netflix, and Amazon.

I hate feeling stupid, so when I know I should do something, and I'm not sure how, I slip into procrastination mode. Usually, the terrible thing isn't so hard, and I figure it out by asking The Google. For those who hate math, I guess even the simplest math chore can send them into a three-day binge-watching spree to avoid learning how it's done.

For example, if you spent $138 on an advertising campaign, and you had a net revenue of $150 what would your ROI (Return-on-Investment) be?

Some people will know this right away, but mathphobes might say, *I made a profit so who cares*?

The people who want to make offensive amounts of money from their books' sales, that's who.

The reason ROI is important is that it standardizes results, so they are easy to compare. If one has run two hundred ads through a venue like Facebook, Instagram, or Twitter over a period of three months, and they want to up their spend (that's prosperous-writer-speak for "increase how much they are spending on advertising"), being able to compare the results of each advertisement is key.

So, how do you calculate ROI? It's easy, and there are only two bits of information you need. How much did you spend, and how much revenue came in? In the case of Amazon, this is your share of the sale, 70% or 35%. (Yes, I know ROI is really based on how much *additional* revenue came in due to that investment, but you're getting ahead of yourself. We'll cover that in a later chapter. Let's keep it simple for now.)

So, in the previous example, we had a pile of money equal to $150. Now, take your little calculator and subtract the pile of money you spent, $138. You can do that, can't you?

So, there was $12.00 profit. That was easy to find, and nobody died in the process. Now, you simply take the profit and divide it by the first pile of money you spent (invested), which is $138.

Seriously, stop rolling your eyes. Punch 12 into the calculator, hit divide, and then type in 138 and hit the equals button. You'll get 0.08695652. Then, if you just move the decimal point two spots to the right, you'll have 8.69 and then throw one of those fancy pants percent signs on it, and you get 8.69% ROI. (8.7% if you enjoy rounding.)

It doesn't seem like a big number, but what if that ad campaign only ran for one day? What if you could take all the money you got from that ad and put it into an ad the next day and make another 8.7%, what would that be after 90-days?

You'd be trying to figure out how to spend over $190,000 on day 91. That's a good problem to have.

So, if you don't like math, that's fine, but you can still learn a little if it means huge piles of money, can't you?

Remember ROI is the pile of money made minus the pile of money spent, and then that number is divided by the pile of money spent. If you start calculating ROI on things you do, you'll have that formula down far quicker than you'd imagine.

There's one more thing. If you hate math and don't even know your times table up through ten, then learn it. Multiplication is the building block for *everything*, and if you don't know what seven times eight equals in your head, then it's time you learn. Data analysis requires being able to spot things that jump out as "unusual" or "wrong." I'm not kidding; learn it, it's only 100 numbers. Memorize that beast. I'm sure you can even find an app to do it...probably on your eight-year-old's tablet. Don't tell anyone, just learn that table!

Learning these things can mean making a lot of money or avoiding making a decision that will cost you a bunch.

Now, let's get to the fun stuff.

1

CLARITY IS POWER

Before we dive into the *how-tos* of making more money as a writer, there are probably a few things we should clear up about us. Also, there are several areas in which you need to gain clarity that will help you in your pursuit of more cash.

As full-time writers with a full two decades of experience between us in the author business, we've learned a lot of things we wish we'd known sooner—like the day before we started. While there's no return button for us to press to send ourselves back in time while still holding onto all our knowledge, we know our combined experience can catapult you from the rocky road of unpredictable results to the newly paved eight-lane highway of monetary author success.

We love the author business! And there are a few reasons why. Not the least of which is, as Kevin Tumlinson (author of *30-Day Author*) would say: "*Pants are optional.*" Seriously, we can't think of one thing we don't love about writing and about our author businesses. Part of the reason we are so happy is that we got clear on a few things we think you should be clear about, too.

What's Your Why?

Let's start with why. We believe most writers write because they are compelled to write. Very simply, we write because we must. But that's not the only *why*, is it? Nope. Without question, we know you're here reading a book about making more money as a writer because you want to make more money as a writer. But *why?* Not because, or not only because, you have some bills to pay, although that could be a big reason. You can even add "pay my bills" to your *why* list. But in addition to the more general why, we suggest you get clear on your very deep personal *whys*.

Without going too deep down the self-help rabbit hole, without an unyielding *why*, you may be tempted to abandon the writing ship when the sailing gets rough. When it's been too long between freelance gigs, or Amazon changes its price per page read, or you publish a new book and seemingly do everything right, only to have it languish in obscurity you might be tempted to give up. We know, we've been there ourselves.

On the other hand, a strong *why* is going to get you up early and keep you up late. A solid *why* is going to help you say *yes* to writing and *no* to other things, when the other things are darned tempting and or very sexy. So, before you read any further, grab your journal or start a new document in Evernote and jot down why you are writing. Next, write why you must make more money from your writing.

Did you get that down? If not, and you're just still reading along, do yourself and your income a favor and just do it! It'll just take a couple of minutes, and we promise those couple of minutes are well spent.

All set? Great, keep that journal or document handy, and let's continue!

Who's Who?

The next bit of clarity that will be most helpful to you is to get clear on your *who*. Who are you as a writer? More specifically, who are you as a full on, money-making writer? Yep, we are going to suggest you write those down too. Next, for whom are you writing? No, not your kids, not *that* kind of *who*. We have something different in mind, or more to the point, someone. The someone could be the editor of *The New York Times*. Or, the someone could be the middle-aged Midwestern housewife who delights in reading a knotty romance every afternoon before the kids come home from school. The person you have in your mind is your avatar, also known as your *who*.

Knowing whom you're writing for will help you to make those tricky writing decisions (Which way should the story go? What information should I include in my book?), will help keep you focused, and frankly, will help make writing a whole heck of a lot easier for you.

We suggest taking five to ten minutes and jot down your *who*. When you're done, keep reading.

Wait, What?

Next, let's talk about *what* you write. Some people only want to write what they love to write. Some people believe they should write what they don't love to write, if they want to make money. We believe you can do both: identify what you can write that people will love to read (also known as what people will *pay* to read). This is called "writing to market." Chris Fox recently wrote a book aptly titled *Write to Market*, and in it he discusses that somewhat controversial approach to writing. But let's face it, you're not just a writer; you're a business person. Every legitimate business is based on supply and demand, including your very own book business. Writing of every kind is no different. It will behoove you and your bank account to spend some time in serious, contemplative thought before you write. Before you market your services or skills, figure out how to cross the intersection of what you love to write and how you can earn a profit and/or a living from it.

We suggest starting with *What do I love to write?* Whether you write fiction or non-fiction, to be successful and make (more) money as a writer, you'll have to write *a lot*. So, you've got to love what you write. Otherwise, you not only won't want to do it, eventually, you won't do it. Yes, even doing what you love can be categorized as work. For some of us, it's as close as we'll get to a job, and even still, writing is work. Sorry if that feels like a bucket of ice water over your head right there, but it's true. No matter how much you love writing, it is work. It makes sense, then, that you should love what you're writing, in order to rig things as much as possible in your favor.

Having said all of that, if what you love to write is of zero interest to anyone, you won't sell your writing. Enter the concept of "write to market." As we've mentioned, Chris Fox wrote an excellent book about this, and we agree with just about everything he says on the subject. The business of being an author requires forethought, planning, and strategy. The planning and strategy piece is where some writers get stuck, and here is a thought to help: every piece of writing requires readers who want to buy it and read it. To that end, you'll want to do some thinking before putting pen to paper or fingers to keyboard. Ask yourself, *What's in it for my reader?* Every writer has people around them cheering them on, and some of those people are relying on said writer to earn a living from writing so they can do important things like eat, put gas in the car, pay the mortgage, and so on. *What's in it for the ones you love?*

Please take a moment and jot down your thoughts.

Where Are You Going to Write?

Next is *Where am I going to write*? If you're Mark Dawson, before he left his day job as an attorney in London, you write on the train or bus during your commute. If you're Honorée, you write whenever and wherever you can. She prefers an especially comfy spot on her couch, but can come up with words in a back bedroom at her mother-in-law's house, at any coffee shop worldwide, and even, occasionally, by a hotel pool. Just yesterday, she knocked out some words on her iPad (using Dragon Anywhere and her shiny new Logitech keyboard) in front of the elevators at the Four Seasons in Austin while waiting for a meeting to start. Brian cranks out words in his fully-appointed writing den/writing haven and has been known to manage a few words in-between crushing opponents on the tennis court.

Point being, you can write anywhere. You must have the belief you can. Make a short list of *where* you prefer to write your words *and write them on schedule* (we'll talk about that in a moment). But when life gets in the way, you are at this moment given permission to create your masterpiece wherever you happen to find yourself.

When in Rome (or Whenever)

Finally, *When will I find the time* is almost every aspiring writer's objection. We don't believe you "find" it; we believe you "make" it. Honorée's writing sprint earlier this week was just after her morning practice, before jumping in the shower, and before working with a client all day. She had just enough time to squeeze in about 800 words in 15 minutes. She has a recurring 6 a.m. appointment to write, and we suggest you create a recurring appointment in your calendar. If your current schedule is somewhat set in stone, and you can predict when you'll have availability, this will work well for you. If your schedule is somewhat or totally unpredictable, block out times for writing on your calendar at least a day, and ideally a week, beforehand. When you treat your writing as an immovable commitment, a non-negotiable appointment you have with yourself, you will write. And therefore, you will make more money from writing! You may want to check out our book in *The Prosperous Writer Series: The Nifty 15: Write Your Book in Just 15 Minutes a Day*, which talks in detail about these ideas.

Consider this: What gets your attention and focus is what you deem important. We're sure you can agree that what is considered important is what gets done. Your writing is a business, and we're going to dive into the nooks and crannies of making more money in upcoming chapters, but first it's important you understand that you are not only a writer and an artist, but you are also a businessperson. Your writing business will require you to put it at the top of your list of priorities. You can, and you must, not only write, you must work on your mental settings, take control of your calendar, and learn to do the other critical activities that are a part of a successful writing business.

Now that you've gotten a handle on some of the basics of making more money as a writer and gained much-needed clarity, let's explore some of the other exciting and crucial factors that will contribute to you making, earning, and attracting more of the green stuff.

Let's do this, shall we?

2

WHAT'S MATH GOT TO DO WITH IT?

We're artists, creators, and writers, right? Worrying about "math" or "data" isn't something we've wanted to think about, nor been encouraged to think about (or learn about). As a matter of fact, artists are known by two underlying stereotypes: they are poor, and they aren't business people. As we suggested in the first chapter, we believe these assumptions are wrong. Especially today, with the climate weighted heavily in favor of the aspiring full-time writer, this book is going to show you why those assumptions are wrong and how to understand and use math to your highest advantage.

Now when Honorée mentioned this book to a fellow writer (who shall remain nameless, but you know who you are!), that writer scrunched up her face and said, *No math! I hate math!* To which Honorée replied, and Brian was proud, *I used to hate math, too, but now that I understand it, I love it.*

Of course, we use numbers for everything, every day, in all sorts of ways, from how many multivitamins to take to how many cups (pots?) of coffee you need before you can get going. We even use math to calculate how many words we've written versus how many more we need to write. Right? Of course, if just thinking about math or calculating nearly anything gets you about as excited as finding a spider in your shoe, it really shouldn't. And, if you go all the way through this book with an open mind, it won't. You'll realize you can use all numbers to your advantage. Like Honorée, after a bit of time, you quite possibly could be won over and be heard to say, *I love math!* (and mean it).

The first step in upping your comfort level and learning to love the numbers is understanding the various terms, how they're used, and what they mean.

(Please note: if you have a math degree, this section isn't for you.)

We all know what math is, but data can be a small word that strikes fear based on our lack of understanding. When most people talk about data, they mean numbers: metrics (how many books have sold thus far), math (adding, subtracting, multiplying, and dividing to gain clarity), and money (the result of your efforts). When Brian says "data" he does *not* mean metrics, math, and money. Data is just a term that means pieces of information in their rawest form. We'll get into this in depth in the next chapter, but here's a quick example. If you had two days of sales of seven units and ten units, respectively, that would total seventeen units. You would consider the numbers 7 and 10 to be data, but not the number 17, because we arrived at that number through a formula (Day 1 + Day 2). Furthermore, if the seven units and ten units were a sum of the sales for three different titles, then the 7 and 10 wouldn't be data either; the individual book sales numbers would be the data.

Understanding data is important because as your business grows, you'll want to maintain data at the most fine-grained level possible. The data should be kept in their own sheet and referenced through formulas. This gives you the most flexibility when it comes to analyzing your data.

Metrics are the summary, average, mean, ROI (return on investment), and more, of a specific data set. Total sales equal all the sales for a period, be it a day, week, or month. We want to have the sales at the daily level, and then we can create formulas to give us the week or month.

As you can see, math has everything to do with your success as a writer, so it's high time you knew all about it!

3

THE BASICS

The basics include lots of words you have probably associated with math and therefore you may have shied away from them. But imagine Honorée's delight when Brian used the very words she thought were beyond her comprehension to help get more of what she wants? While she wasn't excited about *math* (initially), she was excited to learn how understanding the numbers could help her predict trends, adjust her marketing strategies, and ultimately, make more money. We both think you'll find your delight, too. And, it won't be difficult at all!

This is Honorée, and I'm going to hand it over to Brian to walk you through this part (while reserving the option to interject at any moment).

Let's start with that doozy of a math word: data.

Data

Looking at data, which is the most fun thing in the world, is a bit of an art.

Oh, I hear you chuckling. You don't think it's fun to look at a bunch of numbers in a spreadsheet, but you will, once you realize it is like looking for treasure. Everyone likes treasure.

The way one finds treasure is to notice a pattern that other people haven't seen. Some patterns can be helpful in improving sales. We want to teach you what sort of pattern to look for in your data.

As an example, if you have been running a bunch of Facebook ads—let's say twenty—you're going to have some ads that outperform the others. Assuming that it's just random luck isn't helpful, so it's worthwhile to see if you can find something similar in the ads that might be making them do so well.

I have one bit of ad copy for my satire, *Underwood, Scotch, and Wry,* that I wrote just because it made me laugh. I had no idea if it would perform well or not. This copy has crushed it! I mean super-duper, call-Mom, run-around-the-house-dancing, crushed it. The ROI on this ad varied from day to day between 600% and 800%, which is massive. I had never had another ad come even close to that.

Naturally, I tried some other silly ads. They did fine but were less productive in their results.

Patterns and Trends

You're probably curious what my ad copy was. It's a secret...so don't tell anyone...only you and the hundreds of thousands of people who saw the ad know about it.

"More snark than a snark-o-potumus in Snark Town on a snarking spree."

It's completely ridiculous, but so is making 800% ROI. A month later, I was writing an ad for my science fiction series, and I included the phrase "...with just a bit of snark." Guess what? It was my best science fiction ad. It didn't do as well as the one for the satire, but it did beat all the other ads for those books.

That's what we call a repeating theme in the data. It isn't enough data to be considered statistically significant, but it is enough to form a hypothesis: *people like the word "snark,"* and then to test it.

In fact, there are lots of words that will give one a better chance of getting that person to click. The words will change over time and vary by genre, but some will be more powerful than others. If you can figure out the ones that work for your book, it will be your own pirate gold.

A close cousin to patterns are trends. A **trend** is simply the direction that things are moving. If your sales are trending upwards, it might be beneficial to know why. If they're trending downward, it might be crucial to uncover the culprit.

The thing about trends is they can be hard to spot with daily data because book sales can vary so much from day to day. Two years ago, I was happy every day I got a sale. When I ran a promotion, there would be a huge spike. No mystery there, I spent money on a platform that advertises discounted books, and some people bought. Typically, a book that would have one to three sales per day at full price would have 100 to 200 for a day at 99 cents.

As my readership grew, and I started to get five to ten sales per day on a consistent basis I had enough data to look for trends. Still, the jumping around of the numbers—3, 7, 1, 1, 8, 5—made it hard to tell what was happening. We begin to understand what is happening by calculating a moving average.

The Moving Average

A moving average is a *very* useful thing to know about. It can be used to track trends for sales or ad spend, as both are valuable metrics to track. Again, thinking about running Facebook ads, one would likely see their daily spend jump around just like the sale because some days' ads deliver more clicks than others. If you know your ad dollars are returning a positive ROI (you're finding treasure), then it would be good to spend even more money, because more doubloons await.

Your daily spend and a seven-day moving average of your spend are both valuable metrics to keep an eye on. To calculate a seven-day average simply total up the spend for 7 days and divide by, wait for it, 6.9 (no, just kidding, it's 7). To do a moving average one simply adds the new day to the total and removes the day that is now eight days prior.

It's a pain to do on paper but super easy on Excel. I'll teach you how later.

The point is, with a moving average, you smooth out the bumps. The longer the moving average, the smoother the data, so you could do 14-days, 30-days, or even longer, but one can also have such a long range that it flattens out the line so much that it's useless. I like seven days.

Another fun thing to watch for are **records**. A record is the best day at anything, be it highest sales, highest point on a moving average, most spent, or the high point of any other bit of data you might be tracking. If you are continually getting new "best net profit" days, then you're doing something right. If you haven't set a record in eight months, well, you may be playing too many video games.

These are some of the basics. There are many other measurements one can calculate with Excel that are valuable, but I don't want to scare you. Okay...maybe just one more.

Pearson's Strength of Correlation

When I was a data analyst at GEICO, I used to like to calculate Pearson's strength of correlation for my customer retention data. A simple example might be *If I spend more money on ads, will I make more money?*

On the surface, it seems like the answer is always *yes*, but that assumes that your current advertising plan is scalable without any drop-off in results. A Pearson's strength of correlation is just a way of describing how close a relationship there is between two sets of numbers. If you have a bunch of data points where you've been increasing your spend and tracking how much money came in, you'll be able to use Excel (or your favorite spreadsheet such Google Sheets or Numbers) as to see how strong the correlation is between spending money and making profits.

Pearson's returns a number between –1 and 1. If the result is close to zero, then there isn't any correlation between the two things you're comparing. If it is closer to 1 or -1, then there is a strong correlation (either positive or negative). The stronger the correlation, the more likely it is that there is a strong relationship between increasing your ad spend and increasing your profit.

There are lots of high-level statistical tests one can do, but for the most part, they're overkill for what we're trying to accomplish, which is sell more books. If one were trying to improve the bottom line at Random House (or any of the large New York Publishing houses) and looking at their entire catalog, those other measurements might be more useful.

The point is you can do just a little or get really fired up and do a bunch. Regardless, the better you get at seeing stuff in your data the better your chance of building a sustainable career as an author.

Are you with me so far? Good! If not, go here to get weekly updates and connect with the authors here HonoreeCorder.com/Writers. Now, let's continue.

Data Analysis is About Asking and Answering Questions

The hardest part of data analysis isn't the math because one can set up Excel to do that. The trickiest part about data is knowing what questions to ask, and asking those right questions.

Thinking of data questions is a skill just like anything else. The more you train yourself always to be wondering, the easier it becomes. When I run a promotion, and look at the data, curiosity sets in, and the questions pop into my head.

If my book's ad went out in an email blast and was the third of six books listed in the blast, I wonder if there would have been more downloads (or sales) if it had been first.

One doesn't always need to analyze the data to draw intuitive and self-evident conclusions, either. Just considering how people behave, when one thinks about an enormous group, it's easy to imagine that being first on the email blast would be best.

A portion of the people who open the email will choose to click on the first book. Some percentage of those people will purchase and download the book. And of those who do, some will begin reading right away and never return to the email.

I don't need to know if it is 5% or 20% for this thought exercise to be valuable. When dealing with a large set of data (in the case of BookBub mystery genre, over 3.5 million readers), the knowledge that nearer the top is better than being sixth is enough.

But Brian, we don't have control over where the book runs?

No, we don't, but when comparing two ads that ran six months apart, knowing where the book was in the email could be valuable in understanding differences between the two ads with regards to their performance.

This is just one example of how to consider future events so that one might continually gather a greater understanding of their business.

What are some other questions that I might want to ask myself?

In author forums, one sees the same questions over and over, and those are a good place to start.

> *Is XYZBooks.com a good place to advertise my epic guinea pig fantasy series and is $25 to reach 50,000 readers a good rate?*
>
> *I'm running a countdown deal on my book, 25 signs your imaginary boyfriend is cheating on you, and I was wondering how many days I should run it?*

> *In the first month of my cross-genre (Romance/Motorcycle Death Race) novel, I've averaged five sales per day, is that good?*

Knowing the answers to these questions can make a huge impact on one's bottom line. ("Bottom line" is prosperous writer-speak for how much profit you make, not the concluding sentence of your novel.)

But Brian, isn't focusing on making money evil? Doesn't that mean you're a terrible person who's greedy, wants to destroy the planet, and see orphans starve to death in the streets ravaged by war and famine?

No. Money isn't inherently evil or good; it is simply a medium of exchange. If you've written a story about puppies and penguins battling an ill-tempered mongoose, and people decide they want to exchange their money for your book, then money has done nothing wrong. In fact, it has made the smiles you brought to the readers' faces possible.

Furthermore, ebooks don't require any deforestation, so by selling a portion of your books in non-paper form you're saving the planet. Well done!

As for war and famine, if people are shooting guns, it cuts into their reading time, and I hate being hungry. I love snacks.

And those pesky orphans? Well, if you make a bunch of money, you can donate dozens of Xboxes to them so they keep off the streets, which may or may not be war-ravaged. Nothing keeps an orphan off a war-torn street like a first-person shooter game.

So, in summary, you've been given permission to make a metric boatload of money, if for no other reason than to develop superior gaming skills among the orphan set.

Let's continue.

4

READING THE NUMBERS

Now that you have a basic understanding of the numbers and hopefully have overcome any resistance you have to them, you're ready for the next level. Seeing numbers and being able to read them (and know what they mean) will allow you to do lots of things. Cool things, such as spotting trends, making predictions, and even adjusting what you're doing or not doing—we're talking about marketing, production, and other types of planning. Which all eventually lead to—yup, you guessed it—making more money.

Reading and understanding the numbers is obviously Brian's area of expertise, so he's going to take it from here.

How Can Numbers Help You?

There are so many things we can learn from asking questions of our numbers and making sense of the data. It's the questions that then lead to a better understanding of the book business world, and the ones who have that understanding are at a huge competitive advantage to those who are just guessing their way through.

Case Study: Advertising Venues Change

In 2013, there was a place one could advertise their books when they were on sale for 99 cents that did well for me. They charged 25% of the net profit (which they tracked through their affiliate link) so no matter how many books you sold you were in the black.

I had run three ads through them for three different books in my mystery series, and all three had yielded around 200 sales. My profit on a 99-cent book was 35 cents, after Amazon got their cut. 200×0.35 = $70. The advertising venue took 25% of that ($17.50) which left me with $52.50.

The ads got me new readers, some of whom would go on to read other books of mine, so the actual profit from the ads was even better than the $103.50.

I had dozens of author friends who all used this service and had similar results. The venue had over a half-million followers on Facebook, and they could move the needle. In fact, we all considered this venue to be the best one beyond BookBub.

The first week of December 2013, the ads running on this site stopped working.

It was baffling to all of my author friends. They would run an ad, and it would fail to deliver even 10% of what their previous ads had done. Then they would try another. Now, they didn't lose money because of the 25% rule, but they also didn't have any idea why.

Soon, this venue changed their policy and went to a flat fee model. The sudden downturn in the effectiveness of the ads had wiped out their revenue stream.

This is where it's important to understand the "*why*" of it all. For the authors who hadn't used this venue in a while, they had no idea they had lost their effectiveness and gladly paid the flat fee only to lose money. For the authors who had noticed a low performing ad or two, but chalked it up to "bad luck" or "day of the week" or some other theory unsupported by data, they kept pouring their money into ads hoping it would get back to the way it was before.

I knew immediately what the problem was because I think like a data person. I knew that this venue relied on the people who followed their Facebook page, and I read a lot of blogs about the state of social media. The first week in December 2013, Facebook all but killed organic reach for posts.

Before Facebook's change, a post to the venue's page (which was the "advertisement") would reach around 40% of the over half-million people who had "liked" this venue's Facebook page, or around 200,000 people. Overnight that number of people reached dropped to less than 10,000 people. You don't need to be a data guru to see the problem when you understand what's going on behind the scenes.

The venue was dead in the water, and there wasn't an easy solution. They have since worked hard to shift their fans to an email list, but it is a slow process. It is far more difficult to get someone to subscribe to a list than it is to hit "like" on a page.

I never ran an ad with them after the first week in December because I had a theory it would be ineffective. I verified the theory by talking to other authors about their results. My understanding of my past data (and that of other authors) and the current state of affairs with Facebook saved me from spending money on ads that wouldn't have had a positive ROI.

Not losing money is as important as making money when it comes to advertising.

How to Use the Numbers to Make Decisions, or Danger: Erroneous Conclusions can be Expensive

It's important to understand the difference between hypothesis and reliable theory. If one has an idea for something that might increase sales, and they try it once, and it does, that doesn't mean they have an established theory; it means they have one successful test.

Be careful when making massive changes to your business based on incomplete data.

Case Study: CPC Giddiness Gone Awry

Some advertising venues (for example, Facebook and Instagram) allow one to run ads on a cost-per-click (CPC) basis, where the advertiser pays each time someone clicks on the ad. They also allow one to run ads on a cost-per-thousand (CPM, the "M" is Latin number equivalent for 1,000) basis, where the person advertising (you) is charged for every 1,000 impressions, or every time the ad is shown to 1,000 people. These are the two basic models for running ads on these venues.

In one instance, another author friend of mine and I were testing out some strategies. We were using the CPC model and bidding how much we would be willing to pay for clicks. If one bids too low, then the ad won't get shown to anyone because there is someone else bidding more and Facebook will choose to show that ad.

I had been running my test for a couple of months and learning all sorts of interesting things. My friend decided he wanted to give it a go, too. He writes in a different genre from the five I write in, so we both knew that my data wouldn't necessarily translate into how he should bid.

After trying a couple of ads for a few days using my bids, he decided to increase his bid because he wasn't getting any impressions. That's a reasonable thing to do. He started to get impressions and stayed with the higher bid. This means that every time someone clicks on his ads he is spending more than if they clicked on mine, but it seemed it was necessary.

As is sometimes the case, advertising venues change or get more competitive, and this seemed to be happening to us. Our impressions for our ads dropped considerably over a four-week period.

We both decided that we had plenty of margin and increasing the bid some would be reasonable. I increased the bid on about 30% of my ads, leaving the other 70% as the control group. I made sure that I had some ads from each of my books at both the new and old bids.

My friend did the same thing, for a few days.

He immediately saw a huge spike in impressions and decided to change all of his ads.

He is now spending more per click, and that's cutting into his margin. But if it's generating more impressions as a result, then that's a smart move.

Here's the problem: he didn't have enough data.

I left mine just the way they were for about a month. At the end of that time I had seen some ads with incredible spikes in impressions, but here is the important part, I saw them in both groups (old bid and new bid).

With four weeks of data, I concluded that the increase in our bids had zero impact on the number of impressions that were being delivered. The ads that were at the old, lower, bid had just as likely a chance of catching fire as the ads with the higher bid and lower profit margin.

The conclusion is that there was something else going on at the venue that was causing the fluctuation in impressions (which leads to clicks), and though we didn't know what it was, we did know that spending more per click wasn't helping.

If I had changed all my ads, I might have drawn the same conclusion as my friend and ended up staying at that higher bid well into the future. This would have eaten up a lot of my profits without being necessary at all.

Jumping to conclusions is easy to do. I've seen this countless times in forums of people who are working on Facebook ads. They try an ad for three days and conclude it is doing well or awful. I would bet that 95% of new advertisers on Facebook decide if an ad is working within 72-hours of its approval. Those people then make decisions based on that limited data.

I consider all the data from the first seven days to be questionable. I never make decisions based upon the early results for several reasons.

1. I don't know if there is a lag in the reporting of impressions, clicks, and spend. Often there *is* a lag, and if this is the case, one needs to

compare results from Wednesday with sales from Monday. Assuming that the reporting data are always real-time is foolish, even if sometimes it's pretty close.

2. Some ads don't get queued up to start running, even if they've been approved, for a few days (or sometimes a few weeks). If an ad isn't generating any impressions the first three days, that doesn't mean it doesn't work. I've had ads that started generating impressions some time between day seven and twenty-one and then turned out to be rather effective. If an ad isn't yielding impressions it doesn't cost you anything, so why not let it sit for a while? Many authors are too quick to terminate ads that don't work.
3. Different days of the week matter. I want to see how an ad does across several weeks to get a true feel for its potential.

It should be noted that once an ad is generating clicks, it's costing you money and being patient when an ad seems to be generating little return can be hard. Each person must find their threshold for pain. That being said, though, at the very least don't be too quick to pull ads that are just sitting there doing nothing, because they do not cost you a dime.

Beware of False Signs

Once your mind has started to think like a data analyst, you may accidentally start to draw inferences that lead to erroneous conclusions.

I don't always see the forest for the trees. Despite loving data and training myself to look for opportunities, I still missed a great opportunity.

It cost me $60,000 over the last twelve months.

My blind spot was the book description. I hated writing them. They were always the last thing I did before hitting publish because I found the process mentally painful. Writing a 50,000-word novel was a breeze by comparison to a 300-word description.

Writing descriptions is worse than peas.

The mere thought of trying to improve my description made me shudder. One day, though, my little voice said, "You've spent countless hours analyzing your advertising copy and found that conversion improves with better copy. Why wouldn't it be the same with your description?"

I told my little voice, "Piss off."

My little voice is used to me ignoring it and kept at me. Eventually, I had to consider the value of copywriting and the fact that I am *not* a trained copywriter.

This meant one thing. I had to learn about the art of copywriting or hire a proper copywriter. For most people, it may be a smart financial move to spend the money for a professional, but part of the reason I like to learn things myself is for the data.

I knew I'd want to run tests and the thought of waiting on someone else to get the next bit of copy done just didn't work for me. I dropped everything and started to read up on the art of copywriting.

The first book was the *Adweek Copywriting Handbook*, which I can't recommend enough. It's based on Joseph Sugarman's seminars from the seventies and deals with print ads mostly, but the premise is the same.

The first thing I learned changed my life.

Before I get to that, though, I want to mention a common problem among most authors. We (myself included) tend to think that there is one type of reader who is identical to us. I, personally, rarely ever read the description of a book, or look inside. I read the reviews, instead, and usually quite a few of them.

If all readers were like me, then the description wouldn't have any bearing on sales. Fortunately for humanity, all readers aren't middle-aged, angst-ridden, men with an unhealthy loathing of fruit in Jell-O.

And all readers aren't like you.

We authors make far too many decisions based on our gut. Our gut doesn't have much data and only cares about the next time it's going to get bacon. It can't be trusted.

The cure for this mindset is to imagine one million people of all ages, races, tastes, and hair styles. Just because you don't ever click on an author profile before deciding to give a book a try, doesn't mean that nobody does. In fact, we can assume that some portion of the one million people do click on the link. Perhaps they are interested in finding a new author to love and don't want to buy just one book; they want to find a series to while away the hours.

If you are super price-conscious, it doesn't mean that everyone is going to be the same. In that group of one million readers, a portion of them don't care if a book is $4.99 or $6.99. They'll buy the book they want regardless.

I know, I've gotten a little off track since I almost mentioned the bit of copywriting advice that changed my life, but it's important. You need to understand that there are hundreds of decisions we need to make as authors, and your gut is going to try to chime in on all of them.

One bit of logic that can lead a person astray and seems logical is "This best seller's description is short, so that must be the way to get a lot of sales. Keep it short and sweet because nobody reads those things anyway."

I want you to hear your inner voice when it's making those sorts of proclamations and ask it, "Where's your data?"

There are a multitude of factors that go into a book becoming a best seller. Maybe that author had a friend who knew Bill Gates and recommended the book to him. Maybe Bill sent out a tweet that he loved it, and the book took off from there. Maybe it didn't matter that the description was crap.

That's my point. Try not to jump to conclusions based upon the first thing that pops into your mind.

Now, about that life changing bit of ad copy advice.

The point of everything in the copy is to do one thing...get the reader to read the first line.

It has been proven that most people when confronted with a piece of advertising copy, be it in an email, magazine, or book description, scan the copy to decide if it is worth their time.

They look for clues that the copy may have something they need or want. So, a clever copywriter will have headlines in bold, bullet points, and short easy to read sentences throughout. If they are done right, then the potential customer will go back to the beginning and truly read the first line.

Take a moment and think about this.

Are you familiar with the term "click-bait?" Of course you are, and the reason is that we've all been tricked by "You won't believe what these stars said about their famous exes!"

If it makes you click, even though you know you're being sucked in, it's good copy.

But Brian, I don't want to trick people into buying my book.

I don't want you to trick them to buy your book, either, I want you to trick them into reading the description. There is a big difference.

After I had finished reading *Ad Week*, I went to work on my descriptions.

The first thing I noticed surprised me to no end.

Before I get to that, though, let me remind you, I'm a data person. I'm also tricky. I knew from my data that when I drove people to my book on Amazon, they converted from viewing the book information to purchasing it at a rate between 1 in 20 and 1 in 30. Where I became blind was that I assumed that was the best that could be done. For a year, I drove traffic to my books with descriptions that were poorly written and converting poorly.

Did I mention that I'm tricky?

Why, yes you did. What did you mean by that?

Three times in this chapter I've used a copywriting technique called an "open loop." The last one was just above when I wrote, "The first thing I noticed surprised me to no end." That's an example of a headline that's designed to get the reader to move on because they're curious as to what the thing I noticed was. It's an open loop because I went off on a tangent to introduce the reader (you) to an important point before we get to the answer (closing the loop).

That's why I'm tricky.

The one thing I learned was that now that I had a basic understanding of copywriting technique, the task that I had hated in the book business more than any other, was now something I wanted to do.

Yes, I went from hate to love.

I was excited because I now had a change I could make and measure. If you recall, earlier I mentioned that when I drove people to my book on Amazon, they converted at a rate between 1 in 20 and 1 in 30. This was after I had added: "Praise for..." at the top of some of my descriptions and seen a measurable increase in conversions.

So, what could I do if I wrote a solid headline, used shorter sentences, and focused on truly moving the reader from one line to the next?

The answer is: **Make a Bunch More Money**.

OLD Version

Mitch is facing the real possibility that the woman of his dreams may actually feel the same way about him. He's in love and blissfully unaware of the man who has been following him, a man willing to pin a string of murders on him in the name of revenge.

The murders begin in Italy. Alexis Liao, a former FBI agent, is brought in to consult on the case. After two bodies are discovered, both with the same ATM mark, she knows they have a serial killer on their hands. There are just two problems, no reasonable suspects, and after the first two victims, the bodies stop coming.

NEW Version

Praise for *A Touch To Die For*

"I could hardly put the story down." "The plot is too brilliant to even try to relate, and the characters...unique. Worth the read." "Loved the characters and story line"

Mitch had no idea he was being watched.

For decades, Paul couldn't let it go. The personal slight pecked at his brain just before the quiet of sleep arrived. It fueled his hate. Money, success, and fame almost got him past it—until he saw his nemesis, Mitch, with that beautiful woman.

Mitch couldn't believe he was finally with her. A lifetime of distant longing had faded and turned into joy. The scales of happiness finally tipped in his favor. He thought nothing could ruin his day.

He was wrong.

Paul knew that killing Mitch wouldn't satisfy his lust for vengeance. He needed more. He needed something that would devastate Mitch to the core and last for the rest of his life. Paul would make Mitch a murderer. Better yet, he would make the world *believe* that their beloved author was a deranged serial killer.

Who will win?

Who will survive?

You won't believe the twists and turns in this suspense thriller.

Pick up your copy with just one click.

How did you decide to dip your toes into the suspense and thriller genre?

I had just finished the fourth book in my Henry Wood Detective mystery series and was ready to begin a new novel. The problem was I didn't know yet what Book Five in the series would be about. I know that when I shop for something to read I love looking not only for mystery bestsellers, but also for suspense thrillers, and I decided that a psychological thriller might be fun to write.

Where did you get the idea for your first thriller Kindle book?

The books I enjoy in the thriller genre always make me ask at least one question. In *A Touch To Die For* I wanted to explore what it might be like for a genius to evolve into a serial killer. All the serial killers I can remember are geniuses who seem to know every detail about how to get away with murder. Surely there must have been a learning curve?

What type of reader would enjoy your brand of suspense novel?

My writing tends to be character-driven. I especially like character interaction and am interested in their dialog back and forth. I think I get that from my love of Elmore Leonard. Readers who enjoy clever banter with a side of humor will like *A Touch to Die For.*

This change, which admittedly took several hours to write, pushed my conversions to between 1 in 6 and 1 in 12, with most days being closer to 1 in 6.

Because I have tons of historical data, I went back and calculated how much I had left on the table by not doing this back when I made the "Praise for..." change. It came out to approximately $60,000.

Do you see what I did there?

That was my first open loop, and I just closed it. I hinted at the $60,000 earlier and just now explained why that was the case.

Don't cry for me, Argentina. I'm doing just fine, and that missed opportunity didn't make me sad at all. In truth, it was quite the opposite. I was thankful that I figured out the error of my ways after only twelve months. Can you imagine how much more it would have cost me if I had waited five more years and twenty more books?

You'll drive yourself crazy if you dwell on the past instead of rejoicing in the future. My sales are better now because of the new conversion. Because I'm converting better, my books are staying ranked on the various lists longer, which means more organic eyeballs.

It's all part of the process.

There's another point to take away from this, and that's that everything matters to some readers.

I haven't reviewed my author bio in some time. I don't even remember what it says, but I know it isn't optimized to hook the reader.

I can't stress this enough. Learn how to write an excellent description. Once you do, you'll be amazed at the percentage of books with horrible descriptions. Yes, even of the top 100 sellers on Amazon by authors who are household names, almost all have poorly written descriptions.

When you've come to understand the difference between effective descriptions and not, you'll have a competitive advantage over the other books that are trying to steal away your readers.

At this point, you may be wondering, *How do you figure out the conversion rate?*

That's a great question. I'll show you how to calculate that in an upcoming chapter. But first things first, my reader friend. We must first discuss how to analyze a platform before investing our smartly-earned capital.

5

WHERE SHOULD I INVEST MY ADVERTISING DOLLARS?

Where one should invest their advertising dollars is one of the most important questions an author/publisher can spend time thinking about. It isn't an easy question to answer, but there is an easy way to "do the math."

Don't worry, I'll tell you how to use a few cells in Excel to handle the math part.

The reason it isn't such an easy question is there are other questions to answer first.

"What is the goal of the advertising campaign?" is the first one.

But Brian, isn't that an easy question? To sell books and make money. You remember the game "systemless orphans, don't you?"

Of course, one of the goals of an advertising campaign is to sell books. But many factors determine whether an author is going to sell a book to the reader opening an ad. A couple of the basics are cover design and a clever description. Having reviews that help readers decide is important, too. So is name recognition.

I don't have any name recognition. If I did, I wouldn't need to worry about all this stupid data stuff.

Well, even if you're a *New York Times* bestselling author making $100,000 every single month, understanding the data and asking the right questions can help you get to $200,000 a month. You'd be able to help a lot more orphans and possibly donate a bit to your local guinea pig rescue center. Guinea pigs are adorable. I digress.

Still, maybe you'd like to be a *New York Times* or *USA Today* best seller. Would you like to make it onto "a list"?

No, Brian, I don't want to be a world-renowned best seller and have people sing my praises far and wide. Okay, maybe I do. A little.

Well, that's just one example of a different goal for an advertising campaign. Another is to gain exposure by pushing one's book up the Amazon ranking lists. The higher one is on the ranking list, the better the chance of getting additional sales from people who were not part of the advertising target group. We call those organic sales because they were generated by people's searches, and not by an advertisement. They are a bonus.

Some other reasons for advertising beyond just sales are, author name recognition, series recognition, title recognition, and general discoverability. Many people do not buy a book the first time they see it. The more times a book shows up, the greater the chance the reader will have already seen it before and feel more comfortable giving it a try.

The reason we need to understand our goals is that some venues may make sense for reaching one goal but not for another.

But let's look at the most common reason to run an ad: to sell books. We don't spend all that time crafting our masterpiece just to have it sit on a virtual shelf unread.

BookBub vs. "the Others", "Should I Advertise on ______," and ROI

If you've been in the book business for longer than fifteen minutes, you've heard of the book promotion site BookBub.

For those who have only been here for fourteen minutes, let me explain what "The Bub" is and why they're important.

BookBub is easily the most effective book marketing site available, short of having Amazon take up your cause.

They are the King Makers.

If you spend any time in forums, you'll read about BookBub, and the two most common themes will be that their ads are expensive and that it is impossible to get an ad accepted.

Let's look at the idea that it is impossible to get accepted by BookBub.

It is true that they reject eighty percent of ad submissions. Some they reject because the book in question has a dreadful cover or too few reviews (they like to see fifty reviews) or maybe because the BookBub gatekeeper reviewed the first few pages of the book, and it was so poorly written it made Ernest Hemingway look good. (Yes, that was a shot at E.H.)

The main reason they reject so many books, though, is that demand for the ad slots *greatly* exceeds the supply. BookBub will not compromise the quality of their ads by running dozens of books each day (in each category), because their subscribers want only the best of the best.

The subscribers trust BookBub, and when BookBub sends out the daily email, there is an excellent chance that readers will give the suggested book a try, even if they've never heard of the author.

When I first started submitting to BookBub, I was filled with unbridled optimism that they would surely accept my masterpiece, *Henry Wood Detective Agency*, because it was the *Best Book Ever*. (This is Honorée, and I can attest: The book is *so good!*)

My optimism was quickly bridled via a rejection email that had the stench of form letter all over it.

For a day, I was in denial. I couldn't believe they had said "no." This was followed by a morning of anger that could only be quelled with a liberal application of bacon to my tongue. Then I wrote back and asked them to reconsider, but they wouldn't budge. Depression settled in for the next sixteen hours until I finally accepted that I would need to try again.

These are the five stages of BookBub rejection.

I don't know why they rejected my book initially, but I now suspect it was the cover. My original cover (see below) was a black-and-white masterpiece that paid homage to an Italian art deco artist from the 1930s and subtly gave the nod to the old detective movies of the 1950s.

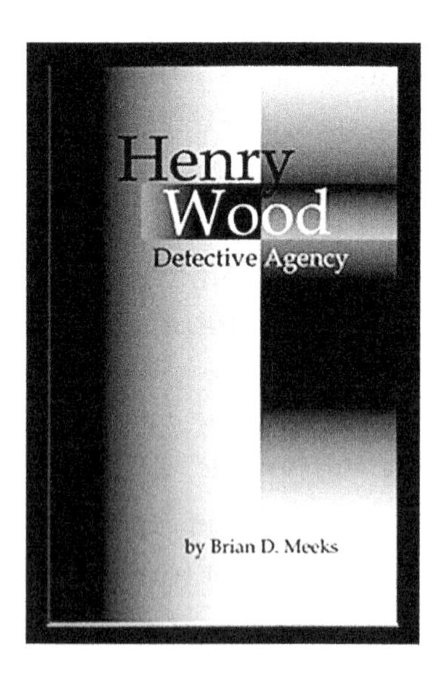

Apparently, the person who made the decision didn't have the Art History/Film Studies degree required to evaluate my art properly.

At the time, though, I didn't ask the question, "Does your cover suck?" because I was quite sure it didn't. I was wrong.

My first inclination was that BookBub might prefer books that were sold in more venues than just Amazon. I went wide and added the book to Barnes & Noble and Kobo.

Taking the bridle off my steed of optimism, I resubmitted after the "please don't bother us again for 30 days" period. They replied, "If you don't bridle that optimism you're going to hurt yourself. *No soup for you.*"

It was 2013, and I was hoping to get a 99-cent BookBub ad. Standing at 0-2 (zero wins, two losses for those whose arithmophobia extends even to sports statistics), I dusted myself off and decided to try submitting the second book in the series because it had a slightly more awesome cover, still with the nod to the Italian art deco dude.

Now I was at 0-3.

The ad, which I couldn't seem to get, cost $600. That's a lot of cabbage for someone who only had three books in their garden, but I had analyzed the price versus the expected outcome and had determined it was worth the gamble.

BookBub provides sales/download data for each genre on the pricing page. I don't remember exactly what the range was for the mystery genre, but I do remember that the average was around 2,200 sales, and since my book was the *Best Book Ever*, I reasoned that if I would get to the average number.

The math was easy. 2,200×0.35 (my revenue per book) = $770. If I spend $600 and get back $770 in sales, that's $170 in profit.

The ROI (Return on Investment, remember?) would be ($770 - $600)/ ($600) or 28.3%. And that would all happen in one day!

More than just the tiny pile of ducats, it would mean that over two thousand people who had never heard of Brian D. Meeks would be reading my book. That was worth a bunch, too.

Of course, I had two more books in the series at the time, and considering this one was the *Best Book Ever*; there would likely be some number of people who went on to buy books two and three at full price, $3.99 and $4.99 at the time.

And then there was the potential organic traffic. Getting over 2,000 sales in a single day would move my detective story into the top twenty on the overall Amazon ranking, per David Gaughran's book, *Let's Get Visible*.

It would also mean my book would rank among the top few books on the sub-genre lists and likely would reach number one.

Surely, with even a day atop those lists, the legions of mystery/detective fans who also appreciate a subtle Italian art deco artist reference cover, would start snapping up my books (and the sequels), launching me onto the cover of *Eligible Author Monthly* and leading to numerous offers of amour from the bibliophile *Sports Illustrated* swimsuit supermodel set.

This was my analysis, and it was only partially flawed. There were no supermodels.

The reality is that one does get a lot of exposure from a BookBub ad, and there are countless numbers of people who have made their way onto *The New York Times* best seller list with BookBub being the driving force behind their ascent.

The important thing was that I was thinking about more than just the $600. In almost every business decisions one makes, there are many more things to consider than just the immediate bottom line. What's the value of a "*New York Times* best seller" moniker? What's the value of a "#1 *New York Times* best seller"?

I don't know the value of either, but I'm reasonably confident that among any group of 1.5 million readers there will be some portion of them who are impressed by authors who have achieved that distinction.

Within that group, there are those who, at least at a subconscious level, ascribe more weight to an author who has reached number one.

Of course, this was all a moot point in my story because they kept taking the bridle off my horse.

I kept trying. After the eighth rejection, there was only one possibility left: The cover wasn't good enough.

I hired someone to create a new cover. It was much better than the one I designed. I then spent $250 to run a test ad, which I'll discuss in a later chapter. That test proved it was a vastly superior cover at getting people to give my book a chance.

This time when I submitted my book to BookBub, it got accepted. I galloped around my house with a joy usually reserved for children coming down the stairs at Christmas. The ad was a success. I was in the door and sure that all my future ad requests would be granted. BookBub loved me.

My next ad request was rejected.

As of the writing of this tome, I've had twelve BookBub ads accepted and probably close to twenty-six rejections. The point is, it did get easier, but rejections are still part of the process.

That's great, Brian, but I wasn't asking about BookBub.

True, but since BookBub is the most desirable, largest, and most expensive advertising venue, I use it as the benchmark by which I gauge their competitors.

In all my BookBub ads I've seen an ROI of no worse than 500% and usually much better.

Because they provide us with a breakdown of subscribers by genre, we're able to quickly calculate the value of their competitors by doing a comparison. Because the BookBub numbers are always changing, I'm going to create a fictitious genre for this example: GP.

Let's say you have a new book in the GP genre, but you've been turned down for a BookBub ad. In the GP genre on BookBub, there are 1,000,000 subscribers. At BookBub's current CPM ad rates, it would cost $260 to run a 99-cent ad, if you were to get one. On average, BookBub tells us that the GP genre generates 940 sales. You know that you make 35 cents for each book sold at price.

940×0.35 = $329, less the $260 to run the ad, gives you a profit of $69.

But you haven't gotten a BookBub ad. You believe you could get an XYZBooks ad. Their ad only costs $20 and goes out to 40,000 subscribers. Is that a good deal?

Well, let's see how much that ad would cost if we paid that rate to reach BookBub's subscribers.

The first thing to consider is that with very few exceptions, most advertising venues don't break out the readers by the genre they prefer, so 40,000 readers does not mean 40,000 GP readers. Some of those readers only read romance, others like detective stories, others want Christian-themed books, and a portion of them want to read about guinea pigs.

But since we don't know the breakout, and we're going to give the venue the benefit of the doubt, we're going to assume that all 40,000 readers are interested in *every* genre possible. (A ridiculous assumption, to be sure, but you'll soon see why that doesn't matter.)

Okay, so if we assume all 40,000 readers like GP, and we divide 40,000 into one million, we are left with the BookBub pool of readers being twenty-five times larger than the XYZBooks pool.

So, if we take the cost of the XYZBooks ad times twenty-five, we get an apples-to-apples (sort of) comparison. The cost of the ad from XYZ Books would be $500 using their ad rates to reach a BookBub-sized reader pool. That's $240 more expensive than BookBub charges. Wow!

But, if one is making 500% ROI at the BookBub prices, then even at the XYZBooks prices the ad should still be profitable, right?

Well, yes, if all 40,000 XYZBooks readers were fans of the GP genre. They're not. It's only a fraction, probably a tiny fraction. If our ad were for a Romance or Mystery book (the two most highly read genres) I'd cut that number in half. For other genres, it might be one-third or less.

Let's redo the math with 10,000 readers.

10,000 divided into 1 million is 100. 100 x $20 cquals $2,000 for an ad at this price to reach a Bookbub-sized audience. Your chances of having a positive ROI on this ad are slim. And that's not even taking into account the possibility that readers in the XYZBooks pool may be less likely to purchase a book than BookBub's readers, which would lower the ROI even more.

So, what would be a fair price for their ad?

That's an excellent question. I could go through the math, but I wouldn't pay more than $3.

It is interesting to note that when BookBub was a young company with a much smaller mailing list, they charged authors zero.

XYZbooks.com wants to make money—I get that—and $20 doesn't seem like much to ask, but if my goal is to make money on the ad, then I'd have to pass.

Does that mean that I would never advertise with them? Nope, it doesn't mean that at all. In fact, I probably would, but only under special circumstances.

6

USING DATA TO MAKE CRITICAL DECISIONS

Understanding your numbers can help you decide whether to enroll in an exclusive program like KDP Select, or whether (as a freelance writer) to write for just one magazine, or even when it's time to go full-time as a writer! Let's look at each one of these in detail.

Brian's got your formulas and Honorée will weigh in with some perspective.

What is the Value of KDP Select Page Reads?

As of the writing of this chapter (note: it changes monthly), each page read by a Kindle Unlimited subscriber nets the author/publisher $0.00537, or just over one-half of one cent. It doesn't seem like a lot, but a KU page isn't exactly like one page of written text. It's smaller.

Because each Kindle user can choose the size of their font, and because Kindle devices vary wildly in screen size, Amazon has created normalized page counts. This number can be found for each book about forty-eight hours after the book is enrolled in KDP Select.

On the Bookshelf, to the far right of your book(s) is an ellipsis (...). Click on the ellipsis and a drop-down box appears. Choose the third option on the list, "KDP Select Info." The next page has all the information about your book, its enrollment period, and in the section titled "Earn Royalties from the KDP Select Global Fund," at the bottom, your Kindle Edition Normalized Page Count (KENPC: Kindle Edition Normalized Page Count) v1.0. For my book, *Secret Doors: The Challenge*, the number is 282. The print version of the book is right at 200, so you can see the number tends to be higher than one might expect.

This means that for that book, if someone reads it in its entirety, the author/publisher will receive $282 \times 0.00537 = \$1.51$. I have this book priced at \$4.99, so this is less than the \$3.45 I would make from a sale.

The question is, would the person who gave the book a try as part of their KU subscription have bought the book otherwise? We don't know the answer to that, but I suspect there is a portion of KU subscribers who only read books that are part of their subscription. For them, the answer would be "no."

To the person who jumps to the conclusion that \$1.51 is a bad deal for the author, I'd have to respectfully disagree. Having a book enrolled in KDP Select offers advantages beyond just the revenue, especially to the newer author who doesn't have a fan base yet.

The obvious reason is exposure because the KU subscriber may be willing to try a book by an author they've never heard of because it's free to them. But there's more to it than that.

The reason Honorée and I love KDP Select is because the page reads metric offers a glimpse into the effectiveness of changes made to a book's cover, description, or if one is running ads, the ad copy itself.

Imagine you're a new author who has a book that sells ten copies per month. That means most days there aren't any sales. Let's say you are tweeting, writing blog posts, and using social media to get people to check out your book, but you're disappointed by the results.

You may be driving people to your Amazon detail page, but not enough of them are hitting the purchase button.

What's the problem? Does the cover suck? Is the description not inviting?

The easiest thing to change is the description, but with such low volume sales it may be impossible to tell if the change is helping to improve conversions.

A Touch to Die For is a thriller and had been out for two years when I decided to spend a little time driving traffic to its page. The book was only selling one to three copies per month, and I was getting a few thousand page reads per month. That's equivalent to another three sales.

My gut told me that the description was crap, so I changed it. The next day my page reads jumped. I didn't have any sales, but a few more people had chosen to give the book a try. This is not significant data, and one day does not a best seller make, so I didn't do any dancing or anything.

Without changing any of my advertising or social media efforts, the page reads continued to average about 35% per day more than before I had changed the description. This increase remained for weeks. I decided to do the test again on my satire, which was easily my best seller, averaging eight to ten sales per day and about 2,500 page reads per month.

The description was reworked, and the next day I saw an immediate jump in page reads, just like with the thriller.

Here's the thing, I wasn't making a dramatic change to the descriptions, either. In both cases, I simply put three quotes from readers at the top after a header "Praise for...:"

That's it.

That single change had convinced KU subscribers to give my books a try at a greater rate than before, and the increase didn't fade. Both books still have a greater number of page reads per day than they did before the change.

The satire, because it sells more than the thriller, also showed an increase in sales, which I think I can attribute to the description change. But I can't prove it. Even at ten sales per day, the numbers are still too small to draw definitive conclusions from, but I can say that overall revenue (page reads and sales) for both books is up nicely.

Making the decision to be exclusive to Amazon KDP Select has not only allowed me to increase my revenue it has also provided me with data that let me better understand my business. The latter point may be the most valuable of all when one considers the life of a catalog of books.

Does this mean one shouldn't go wide and distribute through Apple iBooks, Barnes & Noble, Kobo, etcetera? No, not at all. Like all aspects of the book business, this decision must be made based upon the current state of one's business. The question *Should I go wide?* may have to be asked every three or four months for many years because today's answer may not be the same as tomorrow's.

Honorée here. You must think about your writing as a business. This thinking perspective is actually as important to your author business as your writing. Every business person has a plan and goals and regularly evaluates both. While there are dissenting opinions about enrolling one's books in KDP Select, we believe the best decision you can make is the one you've carefully thought through. Also, you will probably receive advice from multiple sources. Something to keep in mind when listening to someone's advice is to use their own data as a guide about whether or not to accept their advice. For example, someone who has written a few books must have books that sell and rank highly in their categories on Amazon for more than a few weeks or months, and they must have a high Amazon author rank for me to give weight to their advice. I do believe everyone has the best intentions when telling you to launch your book for free, or to "just use any cover," but if they haven't created the author business you aspire to have, think twice before taking their advice. Okay? Okay. Back to Brian.

How Do I Decide What Freelance Work to Accept?

Freelance work is an interesting subject. It can be an incredible source of income that gets one over the hump and into the life of a full-time writer.

Before my books started doing well, I considered going this route but could never pull the trigger. For me, it just didn't make sense because I couldn't get past the idea of writing 10,000 words and then only getting paid for it once.

All the content I was writing would eventually become novels that would earn me royalties for the rest of my life—I plan to live to 350—and getting paid one time for my creativity just wasn't something I felt could do.

Does that mean that you should turn down freelance work? No, it does not. There may be dozens (or hundreds) of projects that you could bang out with little thought because the subject is in an area in which you have some expertise. There are other advantages, too. If the freelance work is going to get you exposure because you get a "byline," then the thoughtful article on "making talking guinea pig movies" might lead to more sales of your book, *Piggywood: The Lucrative World of Guinea Pig Cinema.*

There is also the confidence one gets from writing for others and having it accepted. You may well find you have another level of skill when you're not worried about the piece being good enough for submission.

Though I never went the freelance route, I do think it's a great way to gain experience, confidence, exposure (in some cases), and earn some money. I would *not*, however, suggest you ghostwrite entire novels (or books) for someone else who intends to slap their name on them and profit for the rest of their life. In that case, just publish it yourself.

Honorée again. Brian gives such great advice, and I agree completely with him. There are two other considerations you might want to keep in mind: the number of eyes on your words (a.k.a. "discoverability"), and of course, how easily you crank out the words.

If you can write a freelance piece in a short time and still stick to your regular production schedule (which is based on your tightly-designed plan, right?), *and* said piece increases your discoverability, then I say *Go for it!* The more you write, the more you'll be able to write.

Recently, I had a major platform ask me to write a series of blogs for them in 2017. I have almost a dozen books on my production schedule for the year, and I had to consider whether I had the time and ability to say, "Yes!" (Which I did.) I believe the exposure and additional income is worth the time, energy, and capacity it will take.

When evaluating work, money should not be your only consideration. Evaluate every request with the same set of criteria you would use if you were already fully committed and were making more than enough money. Evaluate opportunities from the position of strength. *Do I truly want to do this? Is it for my highest and best good? Would it still make sense to say yes, if I were already earning a living from my writing?* This is the best place from which to decide. Another thing to consider is how effortlessly you're able to write. If it takes every ounce of your being to work on your long-term creative efforts, and taking on an additional project will drain your creative well, it might not be the best idea. However, if you can complete an additional project without too much of a sacrifice, it might make sense.

Which leads us to the million-dollar question:

When Can I Go Full-Time?

Brian here. I made the decision to leave my part-time job after I had a moment of clarity. Things were going well. I was making about eight times as much selling books as what I made from my job, but I kept going to work two days per week. Part of the reason was that I was using my income from the job to cover my expenses. That left all the revenue from my book sales to be used for more editing, cover art, and advertising.

One day, though, I realized the part-time job was folly, even though I did enjoy it. I had been working on a half-dozen writing projects and had even hired someone to help. As I was working on that "aha" day, I realized I was paying someone $13.50 an hour to work on a project I couldn't work on because I was at my part-time job making ten dollars an hour. I put in my notice that day.

It was the best decision of my life.

I could have probably left the job a couple of months earlier, but I don't have any regrets. I left when it was 100% clear that I was making the right decision. I never wanted to be in a situation where I was stressed out about being a full-time author because I knew that would impair my ability to write. I hate writing when I'm stressed, and I often go into a napping frenzy that could be compared to hibernation, which is not at all productive.

I would wager that you'll know when it feels right. Trust your gut.

Honorée here. I wrote about having a prosperity mindset in *Prosperity for Writers*. I agree with Brian wholeheartedly and think it's important to go full time when the timing feels right. I suggest an income target of 150% of what you need to live. In other words, if you need $5,000 a month to live on, your income target becomes $7,500. From a pure numbers perspective, I suggest you make the leap when you have enough financial reserve that you can weather just about any storm that comes your way. For me, it was having three months' worth of reserve at my suggested 150% target, in this scenario $22,500. I had enough reserve to pay all expected and unexpected expenses for three months (closer to four and a half months without anything unexpected coming up) even if I made no income. Assuming you're already making some income, and perhaps are close to your goal, you won't need to tap into your reserve much (if at all) after you've left your job.

If, on the other hand, your risk tolerance is high, and you're comfortable with "leap and the net will appear," then go for it. I've done that more than a few times in my life and everything turned out, thankfully, just fine.

7

USING THE NUMBERS TO MAKE MORE MONEY

Brian here.

You judgmental bastard, I thought as I saw the middle-aged hipster pick up a book, look at the cover, and then set it down with a contempt usually reserved for domestic wine. It horrified me to think he had just done the unthinkable: He had judged the book by its cover…and found it wanting.

The thing about old axioms is that they survive because of the grain of truth for which they are *axiomated* (I know that's not a word, but it should be).

Test Covers

So you think your cover is good enough? (Hint: it probably isn't if your book isn't selling well.)

Many Indie authors have struggled with figuring out a cover for their masterpiece and often err on the side of affordable. This is a mistake made repeatedly. I know, I've made it.

As I mentioned earlier, for my first book, *Henry Wood Detective Agency*, I had decided I was handy enough with Photoshop to do it myself. I based my design on the art deco work of a little-known Italian designer from the 1930s that I loved. My book, which takes place in 1955, slightly after the art deco period but still within shouting distance, has a *noir* feel, and I believed it would lend itself well to that style.

For hours, I tried different designs until I hit upon the one that I was sure would take the world by storm. I went with my cover, and it was nothing but sunny skies from the reader, and not a sign of inclement weather on the horizon.

Six months later I had had a few negative comments about the cover from people who don't have degrees in Art History and couldn't appreciate my clever reference (including, apparently, the BookBub gatekeeper from Chapter Five). Clearly, something needed to be done, so I hired a professional knowledgable in the ways of art deco. I spent $350 on the new cover.

Here is where keeping data taught me a valuable lesson. Because I track every promotion I run, I looked back at the first Free Day I had run when the book had my cover and then created an almost duplicate promotion for the book with the new cover. They were both done with the same advertising venue, on the same day of the week, and I refrained from changing anything beyond that to make sure my data was as clean as possible.

A clever data person will point out that because I used the same venue for the second promotion, a portion of those subscribers already had my book, so that would skew the numbers in favor of the original cover. I knew this but still wanted to see what would happen.

At 10:01 p.m. on both days I reviewed how many free downloads the book had and the difference in results was telling. April 2013 had 1,161 downloads, and October had 2,589. It should be noted that the venue I advertised with hadn't grown their list much between the two promotions, though it might have grown a little.

The point is that with more than twice as many downloads, the new professionally made cover outperformed the original by 123%.

That is a big number, and one needs to understand that impact it has on one's sales (or free downloads) every single day. A new author is known to nobody, and the cover is the best chance of getting the avid reader who enjoys discovering new writers to give it a try. This is how one gets their writing career going.

It's also why one should keep all their data because, when a change is made, testing the new version and seeing positive or negative results can help with future decisions. Now, I hire a professional for all my covers. It makes a big difference.

Still, it can be difficult to pull the trigger on spending so much money on something we don't know will ever sell. Here's the deal, if you have a bad cover on a great book, you'll never know if you could have achieved your dream because nobody will give it a try. If you have a great cover on a crappy book, you'll probably fail in the long run because the writing sucks, but you'll still have some sales and likely get your money back. Even if you don't, the peace of mind of knowing you gave your novel every chance to succeed will be worth the price of a good cover.

If you're still not convinced, or if you think you'll use the crappy cover until you have enough money for the good one, try looking at it another way. Spending $300 to $400 on a quality cover is probably less than you spent on that high-end golf club or those shoes you just had to have for the wedding. And neither of them will have a shot at producing an income stream (unless you're a scratch golfer or a hooker), so why not divert some of your monthly Starbucks budget to your dream? It will be worth it.

(See picture below)

Original

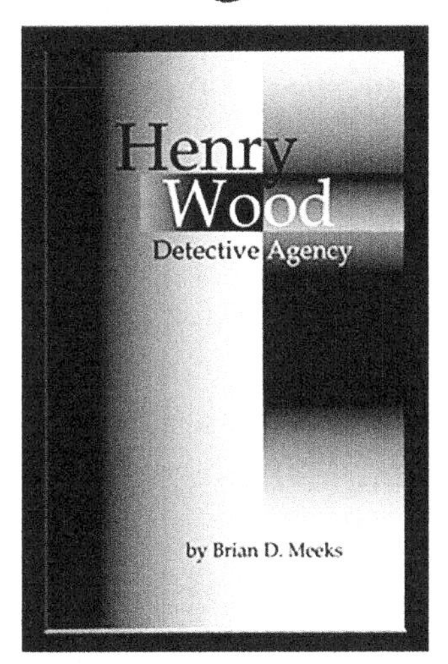

New

Who will win?

Now you've got a Book Bub ad. What should you do with it?

I'm sitting in the Hamburg Inn No. 2 in Iowa City today, eating a Denver omelet and writing. It's January 4, 2016, and a few hours ago, I got accepted for my thirteenth BookBub ad and only my second one at 99 cents. It's a perfect time to talk about what to do after the excitement subsides from reading the acceptance email.

First, read the email carefully. One does not always get accepted for the advertisement they requested. This was the case today. I submitted my book, *Underwood, Scotch, and Wry* in the Literature genre, not because it's literature, but because they didn't have a satire category. It's the genre this book has been accepted to before.

The literature genre has over one million subscribers. My book was accepted for an advert in the humor genre. Humor is a much better fit, and I didn't even know they had added that genre to the mix. It is new and has a much smaller subscriber base (250,000), and the average number of sales per ad is 500.

This is valuable information to consider, and if I hadn't read the email carefully, I might not have known the book was in the smaller category. I'll be approaching the promotion differently than I would have otherwise.

After reading the acceptance and understanding when my ad would run (January 17), I immediately went in and set up a Kindle Countdown Deal starting at 1:00 a.m. on the 17th and running through 1:00 a.m. on the 19th. (Note: a Kindle Countdown Deal is one of the benefits of being exclusive with Amazon. It allows the author to change the price to below $2.99 and still get the 70% royalty during the promotion of up to seven days.)

That's all I'm going to do for this promotion besides gather data on the day of the email blast.

What if it were an acceptance in a larger genre? Would that change my plans?

I write a mystery series, and that genre has over 3 million readers who receive the daily emails. This category affords one an opportunity to try to go for a list (*New York Times* or *USA Today*).

It should be noted that the *New York Times* ebook lists require that the book receives reported sales on more than one venue. This makes their list unreachable for those who choose to be exclusive to Amazon. If one wants to be a *New York Times* bestselling author, then going wide is the only option.

Let's look at how one might approach a 99-cent (or $1.99 or $2.99) promotion if they've got their books on more than one platform, and the goal is to sell enough units to crack the list. This number can be 10,000 for fiction or 15,000 for non-fiction in a single week (Sunday through Saturday for the NY Times). The number of sales required varies from week to week, and certain times of the year require much higher numbers, but we're going to use the 10K number for our exercise.

Ten thousand sales are a bunch. That's 1,429 per day. Hitting that number on the day of the BookBub ad won't be a problem if one is in one of the major genres, but what about the other days? And how does this impact our strategy?

First, the day of the week that your advert will run has a significant impact on the chances. One might think the best day would be Sunday because the book gets a big boost in rankings on the first day of the week and then has six more days to try to hit the number needed for the list.

I would argue that the optimal day would be Monday or better yet, Tuesday.

When submitting your book for a BookBub ad, one can request a specific date or choose the "flexible" option. If the goal is to make a list, then trying to get a particular date may be the best move, though it may also make it more challenging to get the ad.

So, why is Monday or Tuesday better than Sunday?

Having a day before the BookBub ad comes out allows one to try to get additional ads at other venues the day before the BookBub email blast hits. This can be incredibly helpful when one considers the value of the organic exposure from being ranked near the top of the Amazon Top 100 list.

I've studied the results of many Free Day promotions, all of which my book made it to the top three overall, and the organic free downloads unrelated to the BookBub blast make up between 20% and 25% of the total. The exposure is important.

It's equally important, if not more so, for the Top 100 paid list. There are literally hundreds of thousands of people (if not millions) who may be exposed to your book because it's ranked #7 overall who have never heard of you. And with a BookBub ad in the right category, selling the 3,000 to 5,000 copies needed to land on the first page of that list (books one through twenty) is very possible.

Every hour on that first page is gold. The best hours are in the evening after people get home from work. Again, from my data on other promotions I've seen a spike in sales (or free downloads) from the hours of 6 to 10 p.m.

So, we want to ensure our book is ranked as highly as possible as quickly as possible. The thing about BookBub ads is once the blast goes out, and the sales start pouring in, the Amazon ranking doesn't change right away. It can take hours for the next update to hit, and that first jump won't be representative of where your book should be at all. It might have jumped to #708 overall, but that's not as helpful as the next update when it's #57, and the one after that where your precious baby is #5.

This brings me to my point about putting out some ads on other venues the day before your BookBub ad. It's like priming the pump to get the machine running. Right now, your book is ranked 65,287th. Three ads with other venues that bring in a couple of hundred sales should get it ranked in the top 1,000.

This means that after the BookBub email blast goes out your book is already doing well (which may also help sway a few additional buyers to give it a try). But it also means that the first ranking update may be enough to get you in the top 100 by three o'clock, and the next one may land you on that first page just as people are getting home from work. Those extra sales from the ads the day before give one an excellent chance to maximize the effectiveness of a BookBub ad.

It should be noted that this isn't enough, usually, to land oneself a coveted spot on *The New York Times* best seller list, but it's a move in the right direction. The next step is to fill up the days after the ad with as many promotions at other venues as one can land. This is the <u>one</u> case where I don't care about the ROI of an ad and how good a value the price is because the goal is to make a list, and every sale counts.

Given a choice with the other venues, I'd try to schedule as many promotions as I could for the day after the BookBub ad and then fill in the other days with the ones that could give me the date I wanted.

This is also a very good time to plan for a social media scheduled blast.

I hate scheduling tweets. It feels disingenuous to me, but in this case, I'd plan a bunch of pithy tweets to go out once an hour for the entire week. I'd also try to spend a fair amount of time on Twitter during that week. My Twitter focus wouldn't be on promoting the book but just on interacting with people about whatever tickles my fancy. It's good to have non-promotional tweets in one's timeline to make the promotional ones not looks so spammy.

Spending a little energy on Facebook and Google+ can also help. And remember your mailing list. You'll want to explain what you're trying to accomplish in the newsletter because some of your most ardent fans may buy a copy or give one to their friend just to support you.

The one other reason it might be better to be on a Monday or Tuesday is that the *USA Today* list runs from Monday to Sunday. There are worse things in the world than aiming for the *New York Times* list and landing on the *USA Today* list.

It should be noted I've *not* made a list...yet. So, I might be full of crap, but I don't think I am. This business is all about math and data. The bottom line is: the more books one sells in a week, the better the chance of making a list.

This strategy will help you achieve that goal if it's something you'd like to do.

As for my recent BookBub acceptance, it isn't a large enough group of readers to give me a reasonable chance at a list, so I'm focused on maximizing revenue. Therefore, I've chosen the Countdown deal. When one is a member of KDP Select, the Countdown deal is one of the benefits, and when one is running such a deal the author still gets 70% even if the price has been set lower than $2.99 (the point at which the royalty drops to 35%).

There is one more thing to consider, and that's how long to run the promotional price.

When one gets moved up the charts to the rarified air that is the first page on the Top 100 overall, it means a lot of exposure to people who don't know you or at what the book is typically priced. So, it begs the question when should I put the price back up to full again?

If I were going for one of the lists, I'd leave the book at 99 cents for the whole week. All I want are units sold; I don't care about profits.

Since I'm not going for a list with the current ad, I'll be putting the price back to full one day after the BookBub ad. I'd expect maybe 500 sales during the promotion which won't get me to the Top 100, but it will move the book up the rankings of the sub-lists, and that means, to a lesser extent, organic eyeballs.

Those organic readers won't know that the book got to the #1 spot in that category by being 99 cents. All they'll see is a book that looks good at a reasonable price, in my case $4.99.

After earning seventy cents per sale for a couple of days, a few sales that garner $3.45 (factoring in the delivery cost) will be a welcome addition to the bottom line.

Using the Numbers When You're Planning a Series

This section may offend your artistic sensibilities, so be warned. If one wants to find the most efficient path to the day they quit their day job to become a full-time author, then these considerations are part of that equation.

I'm talking about the length of a book. You're planning an epic fantasy series involving wizards, elves, warriors, and battling guinea pigs wielding the screech of death. It will span generations, and millions will die (though not the guinea pigs, because that would be wrong).

Those who read epic series know that each book runs for many hundreds of pages sometimes bordering on a gazillion. That's what you, as an avid reader, have grown to expect, and so that's what you plan to write. The first book will be 154,000 words!

No.

This is a bad strategy from the get-go for many reasons.

1. It takes three times as long to write 150,000 words as it does 50,000.
2. Nobody knows who you are so you'll probably only to be able to charge $4.99 regardless.
3. If you write one book instead of three smaller books as part of a trilogy, you're hampering your ability to do some great marketing things.

Warning: This is *not* to say you should take an existing book and simply chop it into thirds. That is almost always a horrible idea.

What I'm suggesting is that you plan your story to have three great stories with satisfying endings that leave a thread or two unresolved to take the reader into the next story.

Again, I know you're cringing at the idea of writing only 50,000 words. It makes you feel cheap, a sellout, the dregs of writing society, but in an age of short attention spans, people won't notice if they have the next book to jump into.

I did this in 2015 with my post-apocalyptic space opera, *The Magellan Apocalypse*. Inspiration hit me like a ton of muses one day in January. Ideas just kept pouring forth, and I couldn't stop them. I wrote the first book in two weeks. It came in at 50,000 words.

I made the decision to write the next one right away while the first one was being edited. The second book took six weeks because I had fewer ideas, and so it was more of a challenge. It was finished about the time the book one, *Map Runners*, was back from my second editor.

At that point, I made the decision that I'm not recommending as a strategy, but it worked for me. The third book would be written, and then I'd release all three in one month. Again, I'm not saying one should wait, but for me, I was curious if it would help with the launch. I'm convinced it did, but I'm also sure that some people might use that strategy as an excuse to procrastinate. Don't do that.

The point is that by launching the three books on Sept 1st, 8th, and 22nd, I got to see data about the read-through. For this series, I see about 70% read through from book one to two, and about 90% of those who go to book two, also pick up book three.

Now, going back to thinking about my 150,000 words. I could have released it as one book, and there wouldn't have been any read-through. You know what else there wouldn't have been? A boxed set of all three books.

Yes, not only do you get three books, but you get a fourth product to sell. I released the boxed set in late October, and it has done very well. Its price point is $8.99. I would have never been able to charge that for the same book if it was just one book because nobody knows me, but as a collection of three books priced individually at $4.99, $8.99 is a bargain.

Some of you may be wondering about cannibalization of sales by offering a boxed set, and I'll get to that in a subsequent chapter.

Using the Numbers Even After You Think Your Book or Your Series is Done

If you recall, I showed you people *do* judge a book by its cover. This isn't hard to believe, as we've all been bombarded by advertising images our whole lives. I know from personal experience that product placement in sitcoms works, because *every* time I see someone eating Chinese food, I must have some.

I believe I convinced you that a high-quality cover matters. What if I told you that I have just hired a new cover artist to replace the professional *Henry Wood* cover that did so well in the previous example? Well, I have.

The reason is that though I saw an improvement from the first professional cover, I did *not* conclude that I had reached perfection. This new cover upgrade cost $750, and I'll be spending that same amount, or more, on each of the four Henry Wood books. I believe based on the numbers that it will attract more eyeballs than the current one, and that over the long term (you remember I intend to live to 350), I'll easily recoup the cost.

The point is that I recognized an opportunity because I didn't assume the cover was optimized.

Using the numbers to keep yourself on track to achieve goals, such as writing 1,000 words a day for a year equals 365,000 words or the equivalent of six 60,000 word novels!

Author Goal-Setting

Setting goals and tracking results can greatly improve one's productivity. As you know by now, I love numbers. I also like making goals. The truth of the matter is that sticking with a plan of so many words per day is something I've struggled with historically, but I keep getting better.

Don't ever assume that because I'm a full-time author I'm a well-oiled machine. I set goals, reach some of them, fail on others, and am continually trying to improve. It is a constant struggle, but I do see improvement anytime I look back six months to how I was before.

I've written a novel in five hours short of a fortnight (two weeks). It's 50,000 words, does well, and was a fine example of setting up a plan and sticking to it. The second book in the series took six weeks. It was the same length, but I didn't stick to my plan. The third book took around ten weeks. I played a lot of video games during that time.

The thing about habits is that when one falls out of following them, it can be discouraging. However, I've found that each time I revisit the habit, staying with it gets easier, and I stick with it longer. So, if at first you don't stick with it, try and try again.

We've covered some complex ideas and strategies around numbers. And if you're overwhelmed, Honorée can relate. There is a very simple, yet important, aspect of numbers you can start using instantly. It's a very basic strategy: one you probably already know, and may even have used from time to time. The strategy is simply set a goal to write 1,000 new words per day, every single day. Every single day may mean every single weekday, or if you're an overachiever, you may write on weekends and holidays, too. If you write 1,000 words every day of the year, you'll write 365,000 words, which is the equivalent of approximately ten decent sized nonfiction books, or six full-length novels.

If you're following the model of write, publish, repeat, as we do, you'll appreciate that you don't need to write for hours and hours at a time, racking up thousands or tens of thousands of words during any given writing session. When you master the skill of writing faster, you'll be cranking out book after book after book, and getting it all done pretty much before 9 AM. Which leaves you the rest of the day to conquer global domination, or something a little simpler like learning a second language.

Honorée has a simple spreadsheet where every day she tracks the amount of time she writes (usually about an hour, but sometimes only 15 minutes) and the number of words she writes (usually around thousand, sometimes only 500, other days she'll have a word gust of up to 5,000). On another page of the spreadsheet, she tracks the money side of her book business. You can design a spreadsheet that fits your needs, but of course we've provided one for you, and you'll find it here HonoreeCorder.com/m3bonuses.

There are several remarkable things about keeping a spreadsheet. One of them is you'll be able to see your progress. Seeing a child you haven't seen for a long time, it appears as though they've grown almost overnight. By tracking your word count and your income, you'll be able to see and track your incremental growth over time. There are few things as cool as being able to look back and see how far you've come and how quickly you got there in the overall scheme of life. It's especially cool when you got there by doing just a little bit every single day.

8

CALCULATING YOUR COPY'S CONVERSION

Knowing how well our book descriptions converts visitors into purchasers is important. The reason I give a range for my descriptions is that we don't have exact numbers. We need to make some assumptions to get a reasonable approximation of the number. I love precision, but if I can't get perfect data, then I'll settle for reasonable data.

For this section, I think it's best just to jump into some numbers to demonstrate how I would calculate my conversion rate.

For my satire, *Underwood, Scotch, and Wry*, I run ads. Each day I know how many people click through to the book's Amazon page. This seems like an exact number, but it doesn't factor in the organic traffic of people finding the book on their own. There isn't anything I can do about that, so I use the click through number.

I spend a bunch on advertisements each day. Periodically, I'll shut off all my ads for a few days; this gives me a baseline of people that are finding my books organically through search or from having read one of my other books. I have a rough idea of the organic, but for this example, we're going to ignore that piece of the puzzle. I can tell you, though, that the vast majority of the people who visit my book's page are brought there from my ads.

Let's say there are 200 clicks on a given day and we assume they are all from a new ad. To figure out my conversion rate I need to know the number of book sales. Let's say it is ten sales. How many ad clicks does it take to get me one sale? I just divide the number of clicks by the number of sales: 200/10 = 20. So, I get one sale for every 20 clicks. That's a conversion rate of 1:20 or 5%.

But Brian, you said you were doing much better than that?

You've been paying attention. Two points.

Yes, I did, and I am.

Ten sales is not all of the conversions. Remember those KDP Select page reads we talked about before? There are more "sales," and they are downloads by people who are in Kindle Unlimited.

I don't know what percentage of the 200 people who clicked on my ad are KU subscribers, and I don't need to know. It suffices to say that some of them subscribe, and that's enough.

Because I'm not counting organic clicks by people who have searched for a term like Humor and Satire, the ad click-through number is lower than the number of people who actually view the Amazon page. This skews our data to look better than it really is, but that's fine because there is a bit of skewing going on in the number of sales, too.

This is important. The KU readers are real. Their conversions count. They generate real revenue via the KDP Select paid per page system.

Unfortunately, we don't know how many Kindle Unlimited subscribers downloaded *Underwood, Scotch, and Wry* in our example. If we did, we would simply add that number to the ten sales and recalculate.

What we do know is how many page reads we had that day.

Remember when I said "moving averages" were sometimes helpful? This is one of those times. I take the average number of KDP Select page reads over the previous seven days (before the new 200 click ad started running). This gives me a baseline.

Let's say I've been averaging 1,100 page reads on *Underwood, Scotch, and Wry* per day, but with the new ad that number jumps to 3,500. Those 2,400 additional page reads can be attributed to more people starting my novel because they converted.

To figure out how many people it took to get the 2,400 I make a conservative assumption that the people who downloaded the book read 100% of the way through in one day.

That, however, is not what happened. There may be some voracious readers who did just that but not all of them. Some people read only 50 pages, others 100, and one guy with terrible taste read only one page and gave up. I hate that guy.

Still, I need to start somewhere, so if I assume they read the entire book, I divide the 2,400 page reads by the number of pages for the Kindle version (KENPC), which is 300, and I know that at least eight people downloaded my book.

If we divide 200 by 18 (10 sales + 8 KU subscribers), our conversion is 1 in 11.1.

This is why I say the under-reporting of the numerator (200) is offset by the conservative estimate of the KU readers. A more likely scenario is that there were probably 16 people who downloaded the book, which would yield a 1 in 7.69 conversion.

Regardless of the assumptions we make, it is clear that my conversion is vastly better now than it was between 1 in 20 and 1 in 30.

We want precision when possible, but estimates to yield a reasonable understanding of what is going on are still miles better than never doing the math.

What is your conversion?

I can hear you sighing. Is the problem that your conversion rate is fine, but you don't know how to drive people to your book page?

That's a common problem. Let's talk about advertising a little more.

9

ADVERTISING TAKES WORK AND THE PATIENCE OF JOB

(But You've Got This, We Promise!)

Advertising is hard.

It takes a lot of time, money, and patience.

Brian here. As I've mentioned, I use lots of different venues. The most popular is using Facebook ads. This is an incredibly challenging place to advertise and is beyond the scope of this book.

Still, I recommend adding Facebook advertising as a course of study to your list. You may not be ready yet, and that's fine. One can drive traffic using Twitter, posting on Facebook for free, or any of the other social media platforms. I drive some traffic using Pinterest and rarely spend more than $1 per day.

Pinterest is one venue that I intend to investigate further because I believe it could be a reasonably profitable move with a lot of study and work.

Regardless, you should be thinking about trying to find ways to drive people to your page. The benefits are more than just the sales directly attributed to your efforts. Each sale you drive to your book's page helps your book's ranking and is a conversion. We don't know exactly how Amazon factors in conversion to their page ranks, but we can be sure they do.

Better conversion and rankings help your book get discovered by people outside of your sphere of influence (Twitter, Pinterest, Facebook, Google+, friends and family).

The question becomes, how do you know the number of people who click on a link?

There are several ways to track responders:

- Use a link shortener like Bit.ly
- Use an affiliate link
- Send people to a landing page on your website then have a link you can track that goes to Amazon

I try to use more than one because one can't always assume the numbers are 100% accurate. Having multiple data points can help one home in on the truth. All of this requires work. I'm not going to sugar coat it. The suggestions I've made have required many hours of time away from writing.

This may not be what you want to hear. I'm sorry. Don't quit on me. If you can get through the next few excruciatingly painful paragraphs, there is some good news. Yes, that was another open loop.

But the cold hard facts are that my monthly sales are over $10,000 per month because I devote nearly all of my time (95%) to the areas discussed in the book. Only 5% of my time is writing.

That may be a punch in the gut. Understand this: the massive amount of time I'm spending is like building a solid foundation for my writing/publishing house. Each of these pieces, once built, serves me for years to come.

I don't need to learn how to write good ad copy every year. Learning how to track my data only happens once. Gaining an understanding of how to spend advertising dollars profitably is front-loaded, meaning that though I'll need to keep current, it won't take as much time as it did to learn initially.

Furthermore, many of these tasks can be given to an assistant, whom you'll be able to pay from the sizable revenue you've generated by devoting time to your business.

There is one other secret. Once you start using data to find ways to make your beloved book earn money for you, it won't seem like a chore. It's fun.

Now for the good news.

I don't know what you thought about my sales. I certainly know people who make much more than $10,000 every month, but I also know a lot of authors who would be thrilled with that number.

It isn't the number that's important; it's that I've gotten to that point by doing all the things mentioned. Poorly.

It's true. I'm a hot mess.

I've succeeded thus far despite doing a crappy job of implementing my great ideas. You remember a few pages back when I was talking about how I improved my conversion on the book descriptions?

It's a couple of hours work for a lifetime of increased sales. Did I do it for all twelve of my novels and my two boxed sets to maximize my revenue?

No.

I rewrote four of my descriptions, got to *A Touch to Die For*, my first thriller got stuck, and stopped. I could have jumped to the boxed set, or the other books in the Magellan series, which would have been easy. Instead, I bought a new 40-inch ultra-high-definition TV and a new Xbox. This led to a three-day Halo binge.

Before I could get back to the descriptions, I got distracted by another bright and shiny data idea.

That's how it is with me. I figure something out, and it's profitable but don't do a good job of implementation. Nobody sucks at this as much as I do. You certainly don't.

But wait…there's more.

For about three years, readers have politely written me asking when the paper versions of my books would be out. My answer was always, "Soon."

The voice in my head was disgusted. It knew I would procrastinate for years, possibly centuries. About three months ago I started to get some of my print books up. Guess what?

Yes, I started having sales.

Hey Brian, did you do all of your books then?

No, of course not. Hot mess…remember? [Honorée here: I've been telling Brian for *quite some time* that paperback versions of his books would be a great idea. Just sayin'.]

The third book in my Magellan Apocalypse series just needs the cover done to be ready. It would take me an hour. Still not done.

But it gets worse. As I write this, the sequel to *Underwood, Scotch, and Wry* (*Underwood, Scotch and Cry)* is completely done, cover and all. I literally just need to upload it, and the book will be finished. Maybe ten more minutes. Heck, I've already done the ISBN stuff and everything. Just need to upload.

It's been in a holding pattern for over two months.

Honorée here: As of the final review of this book, January 24, 2017, I am happy to report that *US&C* has been published in ebook form and currently has 34 reviews. Please send Brian some encouragement so he finishes the print version in the very near future. Or, before 2027. Thank you.

Back to Brian.

I've found great advertising strategies that make me a bundle of money. For those, I generally do a fine job, but I could list half a dozen things I could do better. Most of them wouldn't take too much time.

Okay, the worst of the blunders has been building my mailing list. This is one of the most important things an author should do. And it should be a focus from day one.

I'm still not great at it.

With every launch, I'm missing out on opportunities because I've not given list building enough attention.

There are more stories, so many stories, but I'm guessing you get the point. You don't need to be perfect to be successful. You don't even need to be exceptional. You just need to pick a few battles and go after them with a vengeance. You'll be fine.

10

THE BEST OFFENSE IS A GOOD DEFENSE

The goal of this book is to help you improve your business and make more money. The goal of this chapter is to keep you from losing years of work by doing something stupid.

Do you know what the most idiotic thing is that one can do in this business?

It has the power to destroy *all* the books you have published.

Unless you've seen this blunder in action, you can't appreciate how quickly things can go south for an author. I mean a rocket-propelled descent into review hell.

The blunder is the rebuttal to a negative review.

The day will come where someone doesn't like your book. It will happen. Doubt me? Go check out your favorite author and read their one-star reviews. The bad review still stings, and I've had plenty. But I never respond unless it is to thank them for their honest review and to say I'm sorry they didn't enjoy my book. Sometimes I even offer another title if they want to send me an email.

I never argue with their reason for writing the review.

This blunder has many forms. Sometimes it starts with something as simple as writing something stupid that pisses off a demographic who is fiercely loyal to another author.

Over a year ago, a woman (whom I won't name) wrote a blog post suggesting that J.K. Rowling should stop writing and give other authors a chance. I read it about an hour after it was posted and shook my head. She was in trouble.

I'm a Harry Potter fan, but that's not what upset me. It's the logic that this woman thought her books were suffering because of one other author's work. That's just ridiculous. Harry Potter fans read lots of books.

This woman wrote literary fiction, was traditionally published, and had several books out. All of them had 3.8 to 4.0 averages on a few hundred reviews each.

What do you think happened when the fiercely loyal Harry Potter fans started to leave comments on her blog?

She started to argue with them. Poorly. This just made them more upset.

If you learn only one thing from this book, it should be this: *Your book is an easy target!*

Within a few hours, her best book had received about ten one-star reviews. The average had dropped to 3.2. None of these people had read her book. They had read the stupid blog post.

If you think Amazon will take down those reviews, you'd be wrong.

I went back a few days later, and all of her books were now below 2.8 average. The reviews were nasty. They were mean. And I doubt her publisher was thrilled that she had destroyed the reputation of all of her works. Also, I noticed the overall ranking of these books had dropped markedly during that time. Yes, sales dried up.

If you keep your eyes open, you'll see one of these stupid blog battles once or twice a year, and the author that tries to defend their work *always* loses.

The author that has thin skin is like a wounded baby gazelle in the open Serengeti. The blog trolls get one whiff of blood, and they descend like a pack of jackals.

Do you want to be eaten by jackals?

I didn't think so.

Yes, it's painful to have someone call your baby ugly, but you need to find a way to cope.

Me, I have an excellent way to deal with the stinging wound. I go to Amazon, look up *A Farewell to Arms*, by Ernest Hemingway, and read those one–star reviews. They are brutal and make me happy.

"Ignore the trolls" is more than just another rule. This is the golden rule of author survival.

Ignoring those that leave bad reviews and not leaving yourself open to unnecessary criticism means you don't want to blather on about politics, either. Go ahead and think of a politician or political pundit who has written a book. It doesn't matter if it is from the red states or the blue states, you'll find reviews from the opposing view by people who live to rant about how wrong they are. Those people can just as easily turn on your book.

When you see a meme that drives you nuts, and the brilliant reply jumps into your head, look away! Do not do it!

Ask yourself, "Am I willing to risk *everything* I've worked for to write a rebuttal that won't convince the reviewer of anything?"

The answer is no.

11

WHAT CONSTITUTES "NOTEWORTHY" IN DATA?

Brian here.

You might be wondering how you can tell the difference between noteworthy data and data that doesn't truly matter? Answer: anything, including data, is noteworthy if it makes you pause and ask a question.

I was planning some Facebook advertising for Honorée's book, *The Divorced Phoenix*, and needed to come up with a solid plan for targeting the ads. This chapter is about the thought process that went into finding my targets. The first thing I did was ask Google for information about divorce rates. I wanted to know if it varied by region or state.

I also wanted to know an age range that represented when the largest group of women get divorced, and as such, might just be looking for a book to help them through the aftermath.

Before I found the numbers I was looking for, I ran across something interesting that I filed away in my notes. January is considered divorce month. I also learned that the divorce rate among people over fifty has doubled in the past twenty years. Again, it was added to my notes.

Forty-eight percent of people who get married before age eighteen are likely to get divorced. That's interesting, but not exactly what I was looking for, so I kept digging.

I kept reading and spotted a paradox. Political affiliation matters in the divorce rate, with conservatives getting divorced twenty-eight percent of the time vs. liberals at thirty-seven percent. Shortly after that, I noticed that the five states with the highest divorce rate were all considered red (conservative) states.

Why is it that the highest divorce rates are in states filled with conservatives, who have the lowest divorce rate? Or, conversely, why do blue states have the lowest divorce rates when they are filled with liberals, who have the highest divorce rate?

There must be an answer to explain the paradox. It was evident that finding the answer would dramatically influence my decisions regarding how I approached the ads for Honorée's book.

The answer was interesting. I won't bore you with all the details, but in short, conservative women get married at a younger age than liberal women. Twenty-eight percent of them will get divorced and then remarry. The chance of divorce dramatically increases with each successive marriage. Their counterparts in the blue states waited longer to get married, and though a greater percentage of the women will get divorced they will stay in the marriage much longer.

What is happening is that in the red states the number of divorces is made up of people who are not just getting divorced, they're getting divorced more than once. So, that's how red states have a higher divorce rate than blue states while liberals have a higher divorce rate than conservatives.

The key for the advertising was in knowing the age ranges that would be most likely to need a book like Honorée's and to plan accordingly. The better the targeting, the greater the chance the person seeing the ad will need what it is you offer.

We are trying to train you to look for things that seem odd and then to dig deeper until the truth is revealed. Also, prior to doing any marketing or advertising, it is important to do market research and look for obvious facts and trends that can influence which direction or approach to take.

12

KEYWORDS "FOR THE WIN!"

So, we've finally got you convinced, and you're ready to analyze something, anything. First things first, my friend. Keywords aren't individual words, per se. They are "word strings," or "word phrases." Although you can use just one word as your keyword, we would advise against it. Here's why.

Keywords are the little sections on the KDP, CreateSpace, and ACX dashboards, consisting of up to seven keywords, designed to help Amazon know who might like your book.

When a reader is looking for a new title, and while they don't have a specific title in mind, they have a genre or topic in mind. They do a search on Amazon (or the other venues). A fan of mystery novels might type "mystery." They might want a specific type of mystery and type "private detective mystery." It's also possible they don't know what type of mystery they want, will start typing "mystery," and then see that Amazon has some suggestions for them: "mystery and suspense," "mystery books," "mystery thriller suspense," and about eight more. Try it yourself: type in "mystery" in the search box and see what else Amazon serves up to you in the drop-down box. We tried it, and got: "mystery books," "mystery best sellers," "mystery books for kids 9-12," "mystery and thrillers," "mystery novels," "mystery mosaics," and "mystery and suspense."

These prospective readers are free to click on any of those keywords, and Amazon will deliver a unique list of books for their reading pleasure.

These readers are wonderful. They are what we call "organic traffic." This is a reader who doesn't know anything about you, but if they should stumble across your book, might give it a try. If enough people do that, you start to build a following that expands the scope of your reach.

Think about this for a moment. If a friend from high school reads your book and shares how much they loved it on Facebook, there will be some of their followers who are already in your circle of influence because you both know each other from high school.

Now, consider an organic reader who lives in 2,340 miles from you and has never heard of your book. If they give it a try and then share it with their friends, you're reaching a whole new group of possible readers (think potentially hundreds, thousands, or tens of thousands of new readers), who are also organic.

The bottom line is: *we love organic readers.* Organic readers are just what an author needs to encourage word-of-mouth, to sell more books, and ultimately (and this is our favorite part), earn a living from their writing.

To help these precious folks find your book, you need to craft killer keywords.

There are some valuable pieces of information to consider as you begin to make your list of keyword candidates.

- Number of books in a keyword search
- Success of books on the first page of that search (ranking)

- Price of books on the first page of the search
- Accuracy of the keyword as it pertains to your title.

Let's Look at the First Bullet Point: Number of Books in a Keyword Search.

Before you do a search, it's best to tell the search bar that you want to limit your search to "Kindle Store." The rest of the advice and data in this chapter assume you did just that.

To find out the number of books that are associated with a keyword, simply do a search on Amazon. At the time of editing this chapter, the keyword "Mystery" returned 15,660 books available for Kindle. "Mystery and Suspense" has 166,234.

Those are two different size ponds. What I mean is that at different points in your book's life, you'll want it to try to be a big fish in a little pond, then a big fish in a bigger pond, and someday a HUGE fish in the ocean.

An example of a keyword that would be considered a small pond is "whodunit." There are only 1,260 books that are returned in this search.

This is where the term "long tail keyword" comes into play. When we mentioned that you are only allowed seven keywords, that doesn't mean only seven individual words. "Mystery and Suspense" would count as one keyword. Each keyword, regardless of length, is separated by a comma. A long tail keyword is a multiple word phrase that is very specific. While it may not match many books, the odds are good that if a reader uses that keyword phrase, they know exactly what they are looking for.

Our goal is to have our books show up as early in the search as possible. Page one is best, page two is second best, page three is still good, page one hundred and fifty isn't very valuable.

The better the result, the better the chance to get organic readers.

Moving on to Bullet Point 2: The Success of the Books on Page One.

We use a tool called Kindle Samurai, but before we discovered it, we manually looked at each book on the first page of the search result to see a few books that are selling well. If all the books are ranked 100,000 or worse, then that tells us something.

It only takes one or two sales to crack 100K in the rankings, so if all the books in a search are below that number, then that is telling me that those books haven't had any sales in a day or two. If none of the books in a search are generating sales, it's probably because there aren't that many people using that search term.

Now, conversely, if there are books that are ranked high, meaning one or two in the category also ranks in the top thousand, and the rest between 1,000 and 100,000, then that's a good sign. It isn't the whole truth, though.

You must consider that there are lots of factors that go into a high ranking. The books on the first page of a search term may be getting lots of sales from other search terms, or from ads, or from people hearing about them on podcasts, or…

You get the idea. We can't assume that a good looking first page makes a keyword term great with only one data point, but we can decide that the keyword is worth adding to our candidate list.

Bullet 3: The Price of the Books on the First Page.

It's easy to get fooled because of "perma-free" books (books that are "permanently free"). If twelve of the sixteen books on page one are free, you'll need to consider whether you want your book that is priced at $4.99 to be competing with all the others priced at zero. It may be a good strategy. There might be people who've grown tired of free books, and so yours will stand out. Brian doesn't have any data on this subject but does know he avoids these search terms (as does Honorée). You'll need to decide for yourself.

There is also the opposite, where a lot of the books are priced at $12.99 or higher. These are typically traditionally published books. There are a lot of people who refuse to buy a book priced over $9.99, so if you can land your book in among these titles, it may give you a huge competitive advantage.

Tip: Sophisticated authors use a strategy called "first free book in a series" to entice new readers to try their books. If readers of the first book like it, the assumption is they will go on to buy and read the rest of the books in the series. This is the "read-through rate" we talked about earlier, and a good read-through rate means you've got a good chance of making a living from your books.

Finally ... Bullet Point 4: Accuracy of the Keyword.

If you spend any time wading through search results on Amazon, you'll notice books that just don't belong. If a person is looking for a cozy mystery, they're unlikely to choose something that looks out of place and instead go with a vampire slasher title.

Yes, it's true that people read many different genres, but we must think in terms of large numbers and build our strategies around that which will give us the best chance with the most people.

Remember, keyword accuracy is important.

Furthermore, if you fudge just a little, and get a sale because of it, but the person wanted hard-boiled mystery, and you delivered a cozy mystery instead, then it may well lead to the dreaded one-star review.

So, now that you have a basic understanding, let's build a keyword list.

Brian is the master here, so let's let him take it away:

Step One: Build Your List of Keywords

1. Open a blank Excel workbook.
2. Click on the tab and change "Sheet 1" to "Keywords."
3. Save your workbook as something like "Keyword Master List to Dominate the World."
4. Now, in the first row put a header. If you have more than one book, it might be good to have the first column labeled "Book title." Make the second column "Keyword."

Since this is the first foray into data analysis, I think I should mention a couple of things I *always* do.

If I'm gathering data that I will revisit and take another sampling, like we're about to do with keywords, then I always include a date stamp in another column.

Then, I try to anticipate future needs for my data.

- Possibly use this analysis for a future book in the same genre
- Possibly use the data to write a book on keywords (which I'm doing now. See what I did there?)
- Use my data to support an article or speech

The point is I include the title of the book I'm analyzing because I may need it later. If you write across multiple genres (or even if you don't), time has a way of making the little details fade, so you'll ask yourself, *What was I researching the keyword "Penguin Antics" for?*

Also, if you have date stamps, you can then combine data from one source with another, say, sales or rankings, and do an even deeper analysis.

Okay, let's continue:

5. Write down the first keyword that comes to mind for your book.
6. Go to Amazon and type that word into search but don't hit enter.
7. Look at all the other searches that are suggested (other search terms will automatically appear in the drop-down box). Those are the long tail keywords.

8. Do any of them look good (i.e., do they directly relate to your book)? If yes, go ahead and start copying them into your Excel workbook, adding each one to the Keyword column.
9. Now, take that first keyword and put it back into search. Add a space, then add the letter "a." This will encourage other search terms to populate. Did Amazon give you more long tail suggestions? See any good ones?
10. You can do this for the entire alphabet if you like.

And your first keyword list is off to a roaring start. Don't forget to hit save.

Now, pick a few keywords that look good and highlight them in your list. Go ahead and do a search on Amazon and check out the first page of results. You are about to do some analysis. Are you excited?

- Click on the first book returned.
- What is its rank?
- How many reviews does it have?
- What does the cover look like?
- Did they use the keyword in their title?
- Did they use the keyword in their sub-title?

These are the sorts of questions that are always on my mind. I'm trying to figure out why the book is showing up on the first page.

Okay, now look at the second book. Is there a vast difference in the rank? There probably is because it's not uncommon for a book or two that aren't selling particularly well to show up on page one for a short while. If it starts to sell, it just might stay there.

The point is that right now you're digging into search. The goal is to see the results as the readers do and to become familiar with what is working and what isn't. The more you do it the more likely you'll start to see patterns.

After spending some time on page one, go to page two and look at one or two books. Keep going through the pages for as long as you can, or schedule another time to devote to your research.

I know, that sounds awful, but it is amazing how much I've learned by sometimes looking at 150 pages of a single search. And then doing it again for the next search term.

In fact, I've become familiar with a lot of books that are competing with mine for the same eyeballs.

There was one author who I'd seen so much I knew what his books are generally ranked. One day I saw his book and checked it, as I so often do, and it was *way* up the charts. I mean, super high, higher than I'd ever seen it before.

The question becomes, *how did that happen?*

My first guess was that he must have a BookBub ad. I went to my inbox and checked. There was the day's BookBub email blast. I opened it, and sure enough, there was his book, priced 99 cents.

You'd be amazed at how often I'm able to make educated guesses about something and be right. It isn't that I've got some special superpower (as far as you know), it's that I'm so familiar with the norm and what it takes to make a change, I'm able to create a hypothesis where others would be just chalking it up to "luck."

Back to the keywords.

I spend hours and hours doing what I described above. It's the sort of thing one can do casually while sports drone on in the background. College football is ideal for research because there's a lot of time between plays and a billion commercials. It makes the research less like work and more like just a thing I'm doing.

Of course, if you don't watch college football, then there isn't anything you can do. You're doomed. Give up.

Not really, but if you cheer for the Ohio State Buckeyes, I'm sure it will help your results. I digress.

Step Two: Narrow Down Your List of Keywords

After spending some time in the search results of your keywords, you've likely found a few that are easy to eliminate. That's good.

Note: It's best to add a column next to the keyword column and indicate "yes" or "no" for each keyword as you analyze it. Most people would just delete the ones they've eliminated. The problem with that approach is that in six months, when you write another book and go back to your list, you won't likely remember the ones you got rid of. You'll run the risk of needing to reanalyze them again. That's wasted time. Always keep your data, even if the answer is "not a chance."

Now, let's dig deeper.

Go back to the first keyword that remains with a "yes" by it. Put it back into search, and in the column to the right of the "yes," type in the number of books in the category.

As I mentioned before, we now use a tool called Samurai Kindle. I like it, but I'm not saying it's 100% necessary. What it allows me to do is put in a search term, and then it scrapes the first page of the search and returns more data. It gives the number of books that have listed the keyword in the title and description. It tells the best-ranked book, the lowest ranking book, the average rank, number of reviews, average price, and there is a "conclusion" column which seems to be based upon the number of books in the keyword search. Often it reads "very difficult."

The tool isn't perfect. The average price is often skewed by free books. Sometimes it doesn't find the rank of a book. Amazon is constantly updating and changing their site to make it better. This means that they may have rolled out a new page design for some books as a test. As such, the scraping program isn't finding all the data for those books.

With this in mind, I can't recommend you get Samurai Kindle because I don't know how effective the tool will be when you are reading this chapter. Personally, I do like it and hope that it is kept in good working order, but I have no way of knowing what the future might hold.

So, you could manually calculate those metrics, which even a data lover like me thinks would be dreadful, or you could come up with some of your own. You might decide to scan the first page and look at the stuff one can easily see, like price and number of reviews. You could have a column that is simply "good" or "bad" to indicate how you felt those pieces looked to you on the whole.

Is that as good as exact data? No, but as I mentioned even the tool I use isn't exact. A "good or bad" rating like I referred to above is still really valuable. The more you use a system, too, the better you'll get at seeing patterns.

Step Three: Categorizing Your Keywords

Below is the breakdown I use for categorizing the number of books returned by each keyword search. You may use mine or create your own. I had reasons for this chart, but you may have better reasons to adjust it for your own use. The important thing is to stick with whatever you choose for future analysis.

- Puddle = 0 – 2000
- Pond = 2001 – 5000
- Lake = 5001 – 10000
- Reservoir = 10001 – 25000
- Bay = 25001 – 50000
- Ocean. = 50001 – A Gazillion (I use 1.3 million)

You can simply reference the chart and then, in a new column, put in the body of water.

If you are feeling extra motivated or are familiar with the "VLookup" function in Excel, you'll be able to create the chart in Excel and then write a formula to reference it. That's what I do. VLookup is a powerful function, and if you spend the time to figure it out, you'll be able to use it a lot in your analysis.

The other beautiful thing about a look-up chart is that if you should ever decide to alter the count ranges, you can do so, and the new body of water will be updated on all of your research. You may decide my ranges suck and want to use your own. If you do a chart, you'll have that option without having to go back and review all your keywords again.

Step Four: Making Some Decisions

You've built a nice little chunk of data, and now it's time to analyze it. This is the fun part. I'm talking "eating bacon at an amusement park" level of fun.

Do you want to be a big fish in a puddle or go for the Ocean?

The puddle will have less traffic. The Ocean will be hard for your book to get to the top.

Here are some things I've learned as I have worked with my own keywords over the last year. I started with a mix of the smaller bodies of water. The idea was to see if I could get my book showing up in the search results and then, when I succeeded (as I'm always sure I will), to change my keywords and try to move up to a bigger body of water.

It sort of worked. It sort of failed.

What we haven't talked about are all the ways keywords help your book. We will do that in the next chapter. Right now, let me tell you what I found with my own research.

There are a lot of people trying the big fish little pond method. What I'm not seeing, though, is that once they've crushed it in the smaller bodies of water, that they're now revisiting their keywords and trying to move into a lake or ocean.

This means that there are a whole lot of authors who are going after long tail keywords that have less competition. At least, on the surface they appear to have less competition because of the book count. The truth is that some of these puddles and ponds are as hard to crack as the larger search terms.

I've changed my focus to larger bodies of water and am having reasonable success. As of the writing of this chapter, October 2016, my satire, *Underwood, Scotch, and Wry* shows up on page 2 row 3 of "Humor and Satire." There are 23,354 books in this search. It's been on page two for over two months. Also, during that time, *Underwood, Scotch, and Wry* has been ranked between #521 and #2000 overall for nearly the entire time.

Is it all because of that one term? No. I do a lot of marketing, but I can tell you that I do get organic sales, and I'm sure some of them find me under "Humor and Satire."

Important Note: Not all searches are the same. If you do a search and find your book on page 1 row 8, then you get excited and call your cousin in Texas and have them do the search, they may find your book on page 3 row 9. The algorithm is complex. There may be a regional component. There may be a bias because you search for your book so often that Amazon knows this.

What I do know is that a book doing well in a term when you search is going to still do reasonably well (sometimes better) when another person does the search. So, don't be disappointed if your friend doesn't get the exact same result.

It should also be noted that when a book like this one mentions a strategy like going for a larger pond, if lots of people have read this book, that will dampen the effectiveness. If the people who had been in the puddles suddenly start splashing around in the lakes, then you may want to move again.

The way I get a sense of who is playing where is the price. If there are lots of 99 cent and free books, those are the hallmarks of beginning Indie authors.

Once you become more established you'll find it beneficial to charge more (not just financially, but because it puts your book in a better class).

Which Brings Us to Step Five: Review!

It's probably not what you wanted to hear, but this may be the most important step. It's one I dreaded doing at first until I started to see some real blunders with my keywords. You need to go back and review your keywords on a regular basis.

I'm going through the review of all fourteen of my published titles and a few of Honorée's titles as well. In almost every book, I'm finding one to three keywords that are just not doing anything for me. I'm not finding my book in the top 100 results pages, so I might as well try a keyword that gets better traction.

The review process will also give you a new set of data. If you used Kindle Samurai and saved each of the searches, like I do, and then dumped them into a spreadsheet, then you'll be able to compare the state of the first page vs. what it was the last time you did the analysis.

Imagine a book is still on page one after a three-month period. *That* is a book I want to watch. I want to read their description and look for the keywords they've included. I want to see if I can find the other keywords they've used and where they rank. This author is doing it right so let's see if we can find out why.

On the other hand, what if a book that was page one, row four, is now on page fifteen, row twelve. What happened?

It will be hard to know for sure, but like everything, the more you get in the practice of asking those questions, the more likely you'll see things that others miss.

Example: At the beginning of the year, I noticed a change at Amazon that seemed to be impacting my number of sales. I had a theory that it was something that would correct itself and predicted to Honorée that around the first week in February, the problem would fade.

I was right, and by the second week in February, my sales were back where I expected. There wasn't anything I could do about it but by having a theory as to why it was happening, I didn't lose any sleep until I knew if I was right or not. If I had been wrong, well, I would have needed to formulate a new plan. Thankfully, I wasn't.

What's Next?

You've settled on your seven keywords and entered them into your book's metadata (on page one of your KDP book details page). Are you done?

Nope.

Amazon is a search engine. That means they are looking for all the information possible to deliver to the screen what the customer is most likely to buy.

This means that the wording in your description may also come into play. If you use the word "mystery" as one of your keywords, why not work that into the description?

You don't want to stuff keywords, though. It might make the copywriting less effective. This would be bad. *Very bad.*

If you have a choice between writing, "You'll enjoy this novel" or "You'll enjoy this mystery novel," go with the second one. You may also start showing up in the keyword "mystery novel," even though it wasn't one of the ones you chose.

Yes, it is possible to show up in searches you didn't expect. Also, it's possible to have a keyword and not show up at all.

I did a test with a keyword that was in a puddle. It was small enough that after the search I went through all of the pages that were returned. You guessed it. My book, despite having that keyword, didn't show up at all.

Conversely, I was researching the massive category Literature and Fiction, which I wasn't using as a keyword on any of my books. Sure enough, Killing Hemingway was on page 150. If you consider there are sixteen books per page, that means that Killing Hemingway was in the top 2,400 of a category that has 1.2 million books in it, and I didn't even have it selected as one of my keywords.

So, how did it get there?

Well, there is another important search component. In step 3 of your book's KDP set-up, you are asked to provide two categories. I had chosen "FICTION>Coming of Age" and "FICTION> Literary."

I didn't even remember doing it, but that is likely the reason *Killing Hemingway* is showing up.

Now, admittedly, being on page 150 isn't generating me any sales, but what if I added it to my keyword list in place of one of the ones that wasn't helping?

What if I worked it into my description?

These are the questions I'm always asking myself, and one of them is how I come up with test ideas. I don't know if I'll ever be able to get *Killing Hemingway* on one of the first few pages of Literature and Fiction, but it's worth a try. And if I do, it will be worth a few sales.

Have you ever noticed how some people include ": A Novel" in their title? *The Girl with the Guinea Pig Tattoo: A Novel.* Well, you can bet they did it to help with the keywords. It's the same with sub-titles. This is another thing to keep an eye out for on books that seem to be on the first few pages of the search, did they include a term in the title?

My book, *Henry Wood Detective Agency,* always does well in the "detective" related searches. I wasn't a genius, though, in planning the title. That's just what I called my book when I started writing it years before I even knew I would finish or publish. I did add the subtitle *"Henry Wood Detective Series Book 1"* as a subtitle.

The rule of thumb is this: Amazon is fine with subtitle if they are A) on the cover or B) an accurate representation of the book. Amazon doesn't want you misrepresenting your book, though, so please try to be accurate.

Double Secret Keyword Idea...

Yes, that was an Animal House reference. Amazon doesn't tell us how their search engine works, so it's up to us to do our best to make the hypothesis and then look for correlations that would give us a reasonable confidence that they're true. We'll never be able to see behind the curtain and prove our results. And the magic behind the curtain will change periodically. But if we have a solid understanding, we'll have an advantage over the rest of the authors.

It seems reasonable then that Amazon may look at the reviews that are left by readers. This made me wonder if I could reply to the reviews and use a certain keyword to help my results.

I tested the theory several times. I can say with confidence that my replies had zero effect. It would be too easy to game if it did, but I still wanted to know for sure.

It does seem like the words people use in their reviews can impact search results. This goes back to what I was discussing with showing up for search terms which I didn't choose.

How is that helpful, Brian? We're not writing the reviews.

True, you don't control what goes into the review, but you do control what's in the title of your book. How many people mention the title when writing a review?

And then here is the secret idea part. When you're reading the reviews, keep an eye open for descriptive terms that keep showing up. If you've never thought of your book as literature, but three people use that term, then maybe you need to do some research and see if you should put it in your keywords.

13

YOU'VE GOT MORE ANALYTICAL EXPERIENCE THAN YOU THINK

It's a Saturday afternoon.

The husband sits down at the kitchen table and takes out his new purchase from the Apple Store. The wife smiles at his childlike joy as she reviews some work reports sent over by mergers and acquisitions.

For a moment, they are both content. He's got his new toy, and the project she's been working on looks like it's a go. The husband looks up at his lovely wife and says, "Are the kids outside playing? It's nice to have some quiet."

The wife looks up from her laptop. Her expression changes. She doesn't move. It's quiet. Too quiet.

"No."

"You mean…" Husband says with a look of fear in his eyes.

"Yes, the quiet, it's coming from inside the house."

Parents know that children of a certain age have only two modes, trouble and plotting trouble, the second of which can lead to destruction most aptly described as thorough, bordering on post-hurricane. Few people survive.

One doesn't need to have formal training as a data analyst to think like one. Your subconscious is constantly seeing patterns and figuring out solutions. The best route to work, the easiest way to get to dance practice and soccer, the rule to never go to the amusement park on the Fourth of July weekend, are but a few of the hundreds of examples of analysis your brain has done without you even trying.

You've got this. We know this because you now have an understanding of math and the other numbers you can use in your favor, and how awesome they can all be! Becoming a successful, prosperous, and full-time writer is essentially as simple as understanding the numbers, and making the numbers work for you.

While easier said than done, when becoming a writer possesses every cell of your being, is all you can think about, and your dream is to make a living from your writing, what other choice do you have but to figure it out? Your other option is to give up, and frankly, we don't think that's much of an option at all. We would commend you if we would take our advice and implement it immediately because that's how convinced we are our advice will work for you. But that would be rude, and we are not rude. So instead we heartily encourage you to heed our advice. To become the writer you've always dreamed of being, to fully understand how to make your numbers work for you, and to share your talents and gifts with the world. And, we hope you'll tell us all about it!

Now go forth and calculate and write!

Resources

LINKS TO OTHER BOOKS IN THE PROSPEROUS WRITERS SERIES:

Prosperity for Writers: A Writer's Guide to Creating Abundance
(The Prosperous Writer Series Book 1)
http://tinyurl.com/ProsperityforWriters

Prosperity for Writers Productivity Journal: A Writer's Workbook for Creating Abundance
http://tinyurl.com/P4WJournal

The Nifty 15: Write Your Book in Just 15 Minutes a Day
(The Prosperous Writer Series Book 2)
http://tinyurl.com/Nifty15

LINKS TO OUR NEWSLETTERS AND OTHER AWESOMESAUCENESS:

The Prosperous Writer Mastermind:
HonoreeCorder.com/Writers

***The Prosperous Writer's Guide to Making More Money* Bonuses:**
HonoreeCorder.com/M3Bonuses

BEST BOOK BUSINESS READS:

On Writing: A Memoir of the Craft (Stephen King)
http://tinyurl.com/SKingOnWriting

Your First 1000 Copies: The Step-by-Step Guide to Marketing Your Book (Tim Grahl)
http://tinyurl.com/First1000Copies

You Must Write a Book: Boost Your Brand, Get More Business, and Become the Go-To Expert (Honorée Corder)
http://tinyurl.com/YouMustWriteaBook

The Miracle Morning for Writers: How to Build a Writing Ritual That Increases Your Impact and Your Income (Hal Elrod & Steve Scott, with Honorée Corder)
http://tinyurl.com/MM4Writers

WRITING AND SELF-PUBLISHING PODCASTS TO LISTEN TO:

Authors' note: There are so many great podcasts, this is not the full list, just a few of our favorites to get you started.

The Author Biz Podcast
TheAuthorBiz.com

The Author Hangout
BookMarketingTools.com/blog

The Self-Publishing Podcast
SterlingandStone.net/podcasts

The Sell More Books Show
SellMoreBooksShow.com

The Smarty Pants Book Marketing Podcast
SmartyPantsBookMarketing.libsyn.com/podcast

The Wordslinger Podcast
KevinTumlinson.com/podcast-rss

The Writer Files Podcast
Rainmaker.fm

Quick Favor

We're wondering, did you enjoy this book?

First of all, thank you for reading our book! May we ask a quick favor?

Will you take a moment to leave an honest review for this book on Amazon? Reviews are the BEST way to help others purchase the book.

You can go to the link below and write your thoughts. We appreciate you!

HonoreeCorder.com/M3Review

THE PROSPEROUS WRITER'S GUIDE TO

FINDING READERS

BUILD YOUR AUTHOR BRAND,
RAISE YOUR PROFILE,
AND FIND READERS TO DELIGHT

HONORÉE CORDER
BRIAN D. MEEKS
with MICHAEL ANDERLE

Digital ISBN: 978-0-9961861-9-3

Paperback ISBN: 978-0-9980731-7-0

Edited by H. Claire Taylor

Interior Design: Christina Culbertson, 3CsBooks.com

Honorée Corder
Brian D. Meeks
Co-authors of *The Nifty 15* & *The Prosperous Writer's Guide to Making More Money with Michael Anderle*

KINDLES FOR VETERANS PROGRAM

10% of the proceeds of this book are being spent to fund Michael Anderle's *Kindles for Veterans Program*. Thank you for helping us to provide Kindles and books by Indie Authors to the men and women who serve!

Special Invitation

Many like-minded individuals have gathered in an online community to share ideas, render support, and promote accountability. When I first wrote *Prosperity for Writers*, I envisioned helping numerous writers shatter the belief that they must starve to survive. I had no idea what was in store, and the result is an amazing community of 700+ writers, authors, editors, and more!

I'd like to personally invite you to join the The Prosperous Writer Mastermind at HonoreeCorder.com/Writers and Facebook.com/groups/ProsperityforWriters where you will find motivation, daily support, and help with any writing or self-publishing questions.

You can connect with me personally on Twitter @Honoree, or on Facebook.com/Honoree. Thank you so much for your most precious resource, your time. I look forward to connecting and hearing about your book soon!

Table of Contents

A Note from Brian & Honorée

To make a prosperous living, every writer and author needs more readers. We need our work to be discovered, bought, and read. And the more often, the better!

We can increase our writing's discoverability thanks to the introduction of self-publishing. Now, the sky's the limit, and we think that's awesome! Although some people moan about the increasingly crowded space, we say, *the more the merrier!* The people who write *prosperity* books are abundance thinkers, right? Right!

The available equal opportunity means more and more people will enter the self-publishing ring. You must do everything you can to stand out, get noticed, and *get your books read.* In fact, we want you to find as many readers as possible who will be delighted by your books!

It's not only about finding new readers. You need to find new readers who will become fans, and a select number who will become *super fans.* A super fan is someone who reads everything you've written.

There are lots of great books about finding more readers, and Honorée has read them all (some more than once), and Brian has spent countless hours in forums, on blogs, listening to podcasts, and testing his own theories to learn what works. We think they are all good and provide key advice you would benefit from. We've even listed our favorites in the Index.

Why is this book different?

The steps we suggest you take to find new readers are in some ways similar to what you've quite possibly heard *ad nauseum* from other successful writers: do podcast interviews, blog, and build a list (all of which you can and should do, as soon as possible). You hear these same things over and over because these tactics are good, solid, appropriate, and effective. Because Honorée has spent almost two decades as a business coach and strategist, and Brian has spent a good bit of his life as a data analyst in the insurance industry, we have a unique perspective and some ideas we think you haven't heard before. Our main objective is to share some things we do that other people aren't doing *and*, hopefully, cause you to *think* and come up with your own spectacular ideas. The phrase "thinking outside the box" comes to mind here, because that happens to be what we do a lot of ... especially when it comes to finding readers. We are constantly devising new, different, and dare we say, *ninja* ways for readers to discover our books.

Going the traditional publishing route hasn't worked for us, but thinking outside the box, going rogue, and becoming finding-readers-ninjas sure has! This book contains the ideas we are using that have worked and are continuing to work for us. We think these same strategies, either as we've executed them or as you customize them for yourself, can work for you, too.

What's NOT in this book

If you do what everyone else is doing (the aforementioned interviews, blogging, and list-building), particularly the successful people, you most likely are going to be successful, too. But there's a limit to how successful we can all be, if we are all replicating the same people. At some point, you will want to engage in some "Blue Ocean Strategy" (based on the book *Blue Ocean Strategy: How to Create Uncontested Market Space and Make the Competition Irrelevant* by

Renée Mauborgne and W. Chan Kim). Lasting success increasingly comes not from battling competitors but from creating "blue oceans" of untapped new market spaces ripe for growth. Said another way, swimming out to a new part of the ocean and blooming there. To that end, we're not going to discuss the strategies everyone is already doing past this point. After a quick discussion about preparation, we're going to jump right to sharing the *other* things we're doing to promote our books and increase discoverability.

Does all of this still sound good? Okay, then, let's go!

SECTION ONE

Your Plan to Find Readers

First Things First

We promise we are going to blow your noodles when we share the ninja strategies in Section Two. But never ones to put the cart before the horse, it would be a disservice to you if we simply shared tactics and didn't help you set the stage for successfully executing them. Section One will help you define your plan for finding new readers, and Section Two contains the strategies that work best for us. These are strategies that will either work great for you, too, or help nudge your creative juices to define some that will yield you new super fan readers. Section Three shares lessons and ideas from Brian, and Section Four has a practical plan for moving you toward the success you desire.

Whether you have a fiction or non-fiction book, why on Earth would you want to go to all the trouble of finding new readers in unique and out-of-the-box ways? Being a ninja is hard work; it requires determination, endurance, strength, and flexibility. We're not in the business of making you guess what works, because we're on the clock here. People must be exposed to you and your books several times before what they see registers. And they'll need to hear about you maybe even a few more times before they act (if ever).

When you play your cards right, put your book into the right hands, you could soon experience the power of going viral. There's nothing like, "You have *got* to read this book!" to encourage someone to read it. But you must get the book into the hands of that first person who thinks your book rocks and should jump to the top of the pile. The reason this is important is because the number one way a book is discovered is through a personal recommendation. The challenge is getting your books in the hands of enough people in order to allow the buzz to occur.

You might not have heard the story of the first book in the Harry Potter series, arguably *the most profitable book in history*. Well, then-single mom and aspiring author J.K. Rowling tried to sell her book to dozens of publishing houses and they all said no. Who's crying now? It wasn't until an agent owed a friend a favor and tossed the book to his daughter, that the book got discovered. Why? Because that young lady voraciously read the book in less than a day, and wanted to know where the second book was.

Yes, dear reader, getting your book in the hands of the right readers who are delighted by it is the ticket you need to find other readers.

THE PLAN

HONORÉE HERE.

I spent almost two decades as a business and executive coach, and coaches are known for advocating for great goals and the solid plans that support their attainment. Now, when I first began, my plan consisted of *identify seven things to do every day to market my book* and I did them. Not much of a plan, really, in retrospect. More random action taken with my fingers crossed.

I missed a very important aspect of a great plan: the goal. What did I ultimately want from marketing my books? Money? Sure! But how much? I didn't say. Sales? Well, duh, but I didn't identify *how many* I wanted, so theoretically I would've been happy with any result, which is absolutely not the case.

I took non-directed action without an outcome because I didn't take the time to think it through. Lucky for me, even though I didn't know what I didn't know, my tactics worked. Lucky for you, I paid the "stupid tax" you don't have to pay! Even without a strategy, I was successful based upon my non-identified outcomes. I made enough money to feel like my time, money, and energy were well spent. But I often wonder: *What if I had based my tactics in some solid strategy? What if I'd known to have a solid plan with action steps based on the goals set forth in the plan?*

You're reading this book because you want to find more readers, as easily and as quickly as possible. In order to do that, you're going to need a plan, a goal or three, and action items that support the goals and the plan. Make sense? Then let's get on with it, shall we?

Your Action Plan

To be truly successful, you need to have what I didn't know to have: a plan that consists of goals and action items. I'm going to walk you through my process for determining my goals and the corresponding action items. I've got a blank, downloadable Plan for you here (HonoreeCorder.com/FindingReaders), and you'll see an example in Section 4.

What Do You Want?

The first step in any action plan is to determine what exactly you want from your writing. If you have a book or book series in mind, knowing your desired outcome is key. There are only two logical outcomes, or goals, that makes sense: you need to sell "x" number of copies, or you want to make "x" amount of money. If you've read my book, *Prosperity for Writers*, you know I advocate for identifying your monthly nut (the amount of money it takes to live your life every month) and then multiplying that number by 1.5, which is your financial income goal. If you haven't yet read that book, you'll probably want to get it to use as a resource and basis for expanding your writing business via expanding your prosperity consciousness.

For your Plan, I strongly suggest you set two goals, one based upon the other. Your financial income goal and the number of sales you need to need to make to achieve it.

I'm going to use $10,000 a month, or $120,000 per year as an income goal. If you've made $120,000 at any point in your life, this probably sounds like a solid number. But if you saw that number and your head exploded, let me present the number to you in another way: $328.77 per day. I like round numbers, so instead of $328.77, we're going to use $330.00 and give you an immediate raise to $120,450 per year. (You're welcome.)

A daily income of $330.00 per day is the sale of just ninety-five (95) $4.99 e-books on Amazon with their 70% royalty rate. You'll need a large catalog of books to reach that number, and it might take you quite some time to write as many books as it takes to sell a combined total of 95 e-books per day. But while the clock is ticking on the amount of time you have to read and get value from this book, there is no shot clock on how quickly you must get to $330 a day, or whatever you've determined your number to be. While, of course, you want to get there as quickly as possible, it will take as long as it takes and I'm here to tell you *it's okay for it to take as long as it takes.*

Goal-setting: Pull out your journal and determine the amount of money you want to make in a year (it could be your monthly nut times 1.5, or perhaps you just want to make enough to take a fantastic vacation every year—completely up to you). Divide that number by 365. (Note: Your income is not taking days off, holidays, or even vacation time. The idea is that you can make money every single day, rain or shine, work or no work … even while you are sleeping! Just choose the number you truly desire to make. Ultimately, it is the activity you take on the days you work that influences the outcome and timing.)

Your annual number is your Goal #1. Your daily number is your Goal #2.

What you've got now are your target numbers.

Action Items

In Section Two, Brian and I give you a list of our best strategies. You can take the best from them and add some of your own. We can surmise you're chomping at the bit for us to get down to it. I, too, am ready for you to dive into it, but there's one more thing for us to cover first.

Your Return on Time Investment

Brian, my co-author for several books in *The Prosperous Writer* series, can ensure that the action items you choose are getting you the best ROTI (return on time investment). Before I hand it over to Brian, let me give one quick example of bad vs. good ROTI:

- Doing a book signing, or even "going on a book tour" sounds like a big, fun, sexy thing to do. The problem is, unless or until you have a private jet and own properties in 50 major cities, you're going to endure an unending string of hotel rooms, commercial airline travel (which, these days, is *super fun*

... not!), and eating all of your meals out. Yup, this is a fantastic adventure for a few days or weeks, but at some point, don't you just want a hot shower in your own bathroom, a home-cooked meal *in your own home,* and to fall into a deep, cozy sleep in your own bed? I know I do! And all of this to sell a few dozen or maybe even a few hundred copies at best. Gross profit: $200-$500. Net profit: less than $0 because you probably have a huge balance on your American Express Card. (Don't leave home without it.) Yup, you guessed it—bad ROTI.

- Doing a teleseminar or podcast interview. From the comfort of your own couch (and yes, you can still shower, eat, and sleep in your own bed with no interruptions, boarding passes, or over-priced room service), you can talk to countless people around the world about your book and why it's wonderful. Someone can't attend? No problem! They can listen with the same device they carry in their back pocket or purse at all times: their phone ... which also happens to double as an audio device that can deliver your interview and even your audiobook. ROTI = *awesome.*

Now I'm going to hand the mike to Brian and let him weigh in with some terrific thoughts I know you'll enjoy:

Brian here.

I'd like to share an ROTI I made recently where the return was actually close to 400%.

Let me explain. I love data and, as such, I'm constantly aware of when I'm letting time slip away. When I've added something on my daily to-do list that I'd rather not do, like, *Write some new ad copy for five ads*, I have an investment of one hour. I can come up with clever copy fairly quickly and I've done it enough that when I see that item on the list, I know it means I need to put my butt in the chair for about two back-to-back episodes of *Archer* (with commercials).

There's a problem, though, a secret time expense that can go unnoticed but is costing you (and me) thousands of dollars a year in lost productivity. I'll tell you more about that in a second, but first, let me tell you what I did to address the one-hour issue.

Writing ad copy isn't as bad as cleaning the gutters (which I always put off until the very last possible day of the fall when the temperature is miserable and the wind is about twenty miles per hour out of the north). It's something that I don't have to do. I could train someone else to bang out the pithy pitches.

That's what I did. I hired an assistant. Her name is Laurie, and she's awesome. She's been writing my ad copy for several months now and, because she has a different voice from mine, has created a lovely new perspective for the ads.

I had originally imagined that paying Laurie to do one hour of my work for me would have a 100% ROTI. I would get rid of the hour of work I needed to do and free it up for something else. I was *wrong!* The ROTI is probably closer to 400%.

"But Brian, aren't you the son of a mathematician? That doesn't seem possible."

Here's the deal. I didn't notice it at first, but when I began transferring the daily list items (ad copy and other things I didn't want to do) to Laurie, I had MUCH more time than just the hour she was working. It was closer to freeing up five hours.

Not everyone who reads this is going to have a problem with procrastinating when they don't want to do something, but for me, it was a bigger issue than I imagined. When I would get to *write ad copy* on my to-do list, the first thing I would do is go get a new bottle of water (or some other bottled drink that I had run out of, because that meant a trip to the store). I'd return with my snack item and check in with Facebook. Oh, what about Twitter? I'd better see if I have any new emails. Wait, stop everything, it's been three minutes since I updated the feed on

Facebook—I'd better get back there. Whew, nothing major happened, but I did see a post making a reference to a movie I've seen a dozen times and just loved. I had better watch it again (now).

Okay, so after a trip to the store, various social media check-ins, a movie, and possibly a brief nap, I'm ready to write some ads. THIS is how I behaved with most of the horribly unpleasant tasks (in my mind) on my list. The moment I had Laurie doing them, I saw my daily productivity go through the roof. I got to work on the things I wanted to be doing.

That's how you get 400% ROTI.

Now it's time for Honorée to close the ROTI loop and get you excited about your action plan.

Hi again! Honorée here.

Sometimes an identified action item that sounds fun and amazing is actually a horrendous waste of time and you'll wish you had made up some lame excuse, like food poisoning or your cat needed an emergency appendectomy, so you could have been spared the torture of whatever thing you're stuck doing. (Or is that just me? Apparently not, after reading Brian's account above.) And, sometimes an identified action item is truly fun and amazing. My point is this: you must not only identify action items, you should do them all while noticing if they are worth your time, money, and effort.

And let me rant about *time* for just a minute. It seems to me most people are confused. They are under the illusion it would be better to spend their time instead of money because they "can't afford to spend money." But here's the truth: they have it backward, and just maybe, so do you! You do *not* have an unlimited amount of time. In fact, I want to thank you for spending your time reading this book, because once time is spent, you can never get it back. Money, on the other hand, can come at any time, and if you're on my prosperity wavelength at all, you believe that when you spend money, even more money is on its way to you. I digress, yet I feel like it's an important point to make. Let me say it another, more positive and less snarky way. *Be doubly as mindful of how you spend your time as of how you spend your money.* You can always get more money, but time is finite, and once it has been spent, it is gone forever.

End of rant.

Now that Brian and I have shared our thoughts on money and time and assume we are all on the same page, let's dive into my favorite ninja tips and strategies for finding readers.

SECTION TWO

NINJA WAYS TO FIND READERS

HONORÉE HERE.

As I mentioned, I engage in all of the usual ways to find readers (the aforementioned podcast guesting, blogging, and list building). When I wrote my first book, I heard Mark Victor Hansen say he and his co-author Jack Canfield did seven things every day to promote their book. And my thought was, *What a great idea!* Not one to, at least initially, try to improve on a great idea, I wrote down the seven things they did every day and did them myself.

While my very first book, *Tall Order!*, was "getting published" (read: being printed), I got busy doing my seven daily book marketing activities. That was in 2004, so I can't begin to tell you what all seven were back then, but I do remember that one of them was to get featured in local newspapers and magazines. I would no sooner do that today than I would wash my own car! But it worked— I was featured in *Las Vegas Magazine* and a couple of other local newspapers and publications and, I won't lie, it was pretty cool. But today, local magazines or newspapers don't exist in abundance, and even when they do, I don't read a single one (or know anyone who does). Just sayin'.

Before I dive into my favorite ninja strategies, I want to tell you why, *thirteen years later*, I'm still making a list of at least seven things to do every day to market my books and find new readers.

The printer I used to "publish" the original version of *Tall Order!* had a minimum print run of 1,000 books. But the cost per book was virtually cut in half if I ordered 5,000 instead, which, being the fiscally responsible person I am, is exactly what I did. Then I had a "holy shiznit" moment when I realized 5,000 books were going to show up on my doorstep (which, as it turned out, was only twenty-seven smallish boxes and wasn't nearly the truckload I thought it would be) in five to six weeks. With visions of my three-car garage turned into a sad version of a storage unit, I knew I needed to get to selling, and fast! Thus, the to-do list of seven things.

But here's where it gets interesting (and awesome). Because I was focusing on finding readers for my books in multiple ways every day, *I found them!* In fact, while the original order of 5,000 was in production, I sold 11,000 copies. New problem: I didn't have enough books coming! Yes, I sold one copy here, one copy there, five and ten copies here, and twenty-five copies there. But I also sold a few batches of a thousand copies, and even received one order for 3,000 copies. The larger orders I sold at a discount, yet I still grossed over $100,000 before I ever saw one book in print. For those of you who are curious about how I sold 11,000 copies, you can read more about this at HonoreeCorder.com/11000.

Now, I'm of a generation that thinks it's gauche to brag or talk numbers. I know some people like to do income reports and brag about how much they are making, and that is just not my style. But I think it's important that I pull back the curtain just a little so A) you know I'm legit and B) you are encouraged to make your own list and get started right away. (Is it working? I'd love to know. Send me an e-mail at Honoree@Honoreecorder.com and tell me!)

Because of my initial and early results with my first book, now, more than twenty books later, I am constantly looking for new, unique, and most importantly, effective ways to find new readers. I don't let the grass grow under my feet and don't think you should either.

I suggest you make a master list of the strategies you can find, and then, one by one, a few at a time (or even seven at a time) give them a try. In fact, as one of this book's bonuses, we've created the Master Book Marketing Strategies List you can access here: HonoreeCorder.com/FindingReaders.

Make sure you give each strategy you try long enough to work, adjust them as the market changes, or as you see them working or not working. Sometimes strategies require some time to take hold, and some you'll have to alter to fit your specific type of book. Some will work better with some books than others. Some will work for a while, and then become ineffective. Pay close attention to what is working, what isn't working, what is no longer working, and see if you can change or adjust them so they work well for you in your book's case.

Brian here.

Before you can continue reading, I think it's important that I mention that *data* is crucial and you will want to track your data so you know for sure if a strategy is working for you or not. Keep track of the marketing strategies you're using and where your book sales are coming from. This will provide you with incontrovertible evidence of what is, and is not, working. And one more quick thing: don't make the mistake of quitting too soon, before you can judge results. It can take several days, or even weeks, before you can truly judge whether any of the strategies you're using are working.

Now here's Honorée again.

Let's Get Ninja

The time has finally come to reveal my favorite strategies. If you've skipped straight to this part (and who could blame you?), go ahead and read. But then start again at the beginning so you are executing from a solid place with an excellent plan, okay?

Here are a few of the "in real life" strategies (a.k.a. off-line) I've been told are leading edge and pretty cool (please note that online strategies are coming up, too!):

Give books away.

The number one way someone finds out about a book they just "have to read" is because someone tells them about that book. I suggest giving away as many books as you can, as fast as you can, as soon as you can. *Tall Order!* is now thirteen years old, but if you haven't heard about it before right now the book is new to you. My point being that even a book that's been around 100 years is new to the person who hasn't heard about it yet. If you have the opportunity to give someone a book, by all means, *give them your book!* Giving away copies of your book can cost as little as a dollar or as much as a few dollars. In the case of my original *Tall Order!* (2004 version) book, I purchased those first 5,000 copies for $4,000, a cost of eighty cents per book. If you're new or just starting out, spending even a few dollars over and over might be too much for your pocketbook to bear. I get it, I'm fiscally responsible, remember? Make no mistake, your book is not just a book; it is your business, or at least a revenue stream of your overall business. To that end, I thought up a few ways to gain exposure for my books that cut the cost to a fraction of a cent in both of the following cases:

Use postcards.

When I published *Vision to Reality* in 2013, I had postcards made with just the book cover on one side of the postcard, and left the opposite side in the same style as a regular postcard. This enabled me to send a postcard and ask the recipient *Would you like a copy of this book?* They had the option of using the QR code on the message side of the postcard to purchase the e-book, paperback, or audiobook directly from Amazon, or they could visit my website (also listed) to purchase a signed copy from me. Of course, seeing the postcard wasn't limited to just the recipient. Anyone who saw the postcard could indeed be intrigued enough to look up the book and get a copy if it was right for them. Since then, I have also had postcards made for *If Divorce is a Game, These are the Rules.* My lovely assistant, Christina, sends out a few a week to divorce attorneys, with the message "to request a complimentary copy of this book, feel free to email Christina@HonoreeCorder.com and we'll be happy to send you one." The postcard is a low cost and effective way to raise awareness about the book, and has resulted in another fun result: large-quantity purchases and even custom-printed copies.

Bookmarks are awesome, too.

For *The Successful Single Mom* and *The Successful Single Dad* books, I created bookmarks that could be shipped along with the original printed copies of the book. Because the book pre-dated CreateSpace, I had purchased thousands of copies and distributed them on Amazon through their Amazon Advantage program (http://tinyurl.com/h4xbnl3). But as luck would have it, I not only changed addresses, I also got married, changed my name, and moved to another state. Not very strategic on my part, and while each one presents its own problem, all of them combined made my head spin. All the contact information (including the website information) listed inside the book became null and void. Rather than creating the world's largest book bonfire, I decided to get creative and figure out a way to update the info without wasting the book. I used bookmarks with my updated information and a QR code and inserted them inside the front cover. The bookmarks also gave a special offer and enabled me to sell the books (instead of using them in place of firewood). Bookmarks can also be mailed, left in strategic places, even used in giveaways.

Both postcards and bookmarks are incredibly cheap. Postcards run about $150 for 2500 (and it takes quite awhile to give away 2500 postcards, even with fierce intention and determination)! Bookmarks are equally as inexpensive – around $25-45 for 1000 at http://waxpaper.interfirm.com. They offer multiple size and color options, as well as printing on one or two sides of your bookmark!

Stamps.

I recently got stamps for *You Must Write a Book, Prosperity for Writers,* and *Vision to Reality*. They are full front covers of both books, made thumbnail size and in stamp form—the cost is the price of a stamp plus a tiny bit more for printing. I get compliments on them every time I use them, and again, they aren't limited to the intended recipient's eyeballs. Anyone who sees them will most likely take notice because unique stamps are rare and eye-catching. You might even find yourself getting back in the habit of writing daily thank-you notes! You can get yours from Zazzle.com (which is one of two providers to USPS.com). They also make great gifts for authors, too.

"CULT OF (INSERT YOUR NAME HERE)" SWAG.

My wonderful and encouraging friend, Amy Teegan, first coined the phrase "Cult of Honorée" and immediately Christina (my director of operations) had mugs made with my company logo and turned the phrase into a hashtag: #cultofhonoree. While I find this hysterical, creating my own hashtag or swag isn't something I would have done myself. However, recipients of the mugs use, love, and cherish them (and post them on Instagram with #cultofhonoree). Which is most likely exactly what will happen if you create some of your own. You could use your book covers on mugs, T-shirts, or even book bags and give them away when (1) someone leaves a five-star review for your book, (2) someone sends you a handwritten note telling you they love you and/or your books, (3) you hold a drawing or a contest, or (4) you have a book signing.

(Brian here: I use my #cultofhonoree mug every day.)

STARBUCKS COFFEE SHOPS.

Starbucks provide their very own unique and wonderful opportunity for authors. Not only can you write there and have snacks and drinks at your disposal, you can utilize them to increase discoverability, *and* find new readers! Have you ever noticed each one has either a lending library or a newspaper basket—or both? When you're finished with your newspaper, you can leave it on your table for the next person, or place is in the basket near the "newspapers for sale" rack for reuse. Well, who said only newspapers go in those baskets? Not me! I don't visit a Starbucks anywhere on my travels (even if it is to one of the two locations that are less than three minutes from my home) without leaving at least one of my books behind. Sometimes if I don't have a book, I will add a postcard or a bookmark to the information board. My local Starbucks love me for it (and always have a Venti Youthberry tea with three Splenda at the ready when they see me coming). I was just in Miramar Beach, Florida, over spring break. Of course, my family headed to Starbucks each morning after breakfast, and, of course, I made friends with the baristas. Among them was a single mom who was so stoked I was bringing a book along to leave behind. If your book is nonfiction, it might find the perfect reader at the perfect moment and provide them with the solution they've been seeking. If your book is fiction, it might just find the perfect reader at the perfect moment who needed to get lost in the story only your imagination could provide. I just got five new subscribers to my list in the past week from Baton Rouge, Louisiana ... one of the places we stopped both ways on our trip. Coincidence? Who knows, but I don't think so!

Seeding the Market

"Seeding the market" is what I call leaving my books, postcards, and bookmarks pretty much everywhere I go. More than two or three *dozen* times I've received an email from someone telling me they stumbled upon my book and usually, at just the moment they needed it most.

Am I making money directly from the books and postcards I leave behind or send? Not necessarily. But is it possible, probable even, that the person who finds the book might purchase another book, one of my courses, hire me as their coach, or even buy an e-book copy of the book they found? *Yes.* All of the above have happened, making my seeding strategy incredibly effective. About two years ago, I sent a box of *The Successful Single Mom* book (box count: 128) with my in-laws on a fifteen-state tour. They drove from Louisiana to Nova Scotia and back … leaving my books at Starbucks all along the way. A win for Starbucks (repeat customers!), a win for Starbucks customers (buy a coffee, get a book!), and a win for me, who found new readers in new places with a relatively small time and monetary investment.

Doctors' offices.

At least once a year, my doctor tasks me with having my blood tested. I leave my books in his office and at the clinic. My husband and daughter also find themselves in doctors' offices (and dentists and massage therapists and nail salons) at various times throughout the year. You can bet your sweet self my books, bookmarks, and postcards are left behind each and every time.

Airports and airplanes.

As a corporate trainer and speaker, I have occasion to travel several times a year. In addition, my husband and daughter are always up for an adventure. And when it's done via the friendly skies, I'm provided with yet more opportunities (as are you!) to seed the market. Leave a book in the seatback pocket, a postcard in the airline magazine, a bookmark in a book similar to yours in the airport bookstore.

Bookstores.

Speaking of bookstores, until Amazon recently opened bookstore number one in Seattle to showcase its bestselling titles (congratulations to my business partner in *The Miracle Morning* book series, Hal Elrod, for being one of the featured titles!), I was convinced brick and mortar bookstores were not long for this world. Now, I'm not so sure. But what I have been doing for years, because I have never been "one of the chosen few" whose books were distributed to bookstores everywhere, is put my books in bookstores exactly where they would be on the shelf if they *were* distributed to bookstores everywhere. Just one copy. Spine out—I mean, I'm not paying for the front cover facing space. When I go back a couple of days later, you know what? Nine times out of ten, the book *is not there.* Either someone found it and tried to buy it, or someone at the store found it and, well, I don't know what exactly. But on dozens of occasions, again, I have received a call from bookstores as small as the mom and pop independent store in Milwaukee, Wisconsin, to the Barnes and Noble I can hit with a rock from my front door wanting to know how they can *get more books.* "Someone tried to buy your book. We're not sure how it got here, but we couldn't sell it and had to let them have it. But we'd like to order some. Can we?" Ummm, *yes!*

FAMILY AND FRIENDS AS YOUR MARKETING TEAM.

My husband, Byron, has an office at We Work, a co-op work space where he rents an office and shares common areas. A few times a week, he leaves any or all of my business books in the common areas or conference rooms or even private phone booths for the next user to find. He also leaves behind postcards and bookmarks at his regular Starbucks. A few of my friends travel quite a bit for work, and for those who are (not yet) authors, I give them a book or two and some postcards to help me with my cause.

Online Ninja Strategies for Finding Readers

Readers are everywhere, and you can be, too. What do I mean? Well, in addition to leaving physical books in actual places, you can leave digital breadcrumbs for your future readers to find. Make sure you do some (all!) of the following action items to find more readers.

Publish in all formats.

While each of us has our preferred method of reading, there are readers who will only read physical copies of a book. People who travel quite a bit love the portability of their Kindle or iPad for taking lots of books along for the ride (and easy and instant accessibility). The newest way to consume a book is, without question, the audiobook—and it is quickly becoming a fan favorite. As the author, you don't have to be monogamous to one format. In fact, it behooves you to provide them all.

Why? Because, as I mentioned, different readers prefer different formats. Some readers like to own all formats of their favorite books! Having your book in physical format is great for those who like to highlight, mark specific pages or passages, or refer to their book. A digital book usually costs less and is portable. Audiobooks are gaining in popularity and with Amazon's Whispersync feature, your reader can read a great story before going to bed, and continue "reading" right where they left off as they work out, get ready, or even drive to work the next morning.

In addition, you are considered even more serious about your author status with multiple formats. When all three formats show up on your Amazon or Apple sales pages, you tell the world, *I am a serious author, you should read my book!* We won't go off on a tangent to discuss how to get your audiobooks produced, but keep this in mind: just as we've advocated producing professional books, we know a professionally produced audiobook is just as important.

E-BOOK–SPECIFIC PROMOTIONS.

While there's nothing quite like giving away a physical book, don't underestimate the power of giving away your e-book as well. Here are just two options:

GIVE AS A GIFT.

Amazon's sales pages offer the "Give as a Gift" function (about two inches beneath the price). You can give the book to the recipient of your choice, all you need is their email address. You can forward the gift email or print and personally deliver it to the recipient. You can also choose the date of delivery (think birthday, anniversary, or the holiday of your choice). Finally, you have the option of personalizing a message to the recipient.

Make it available to all!

Just as I think you just can't lose by giving your physical books away, sharing your e-books can help you find more readers. You can make the book available via a special page on your website, or even in your own website store. And, if you don't yet know about Bookfunnel.com, you're in for a treat. This low-priced option for providing your e-book in the format of the recipient's choice is simply genius. All you have to do is upload the PDF, .mobi, and .epub versions of your book, provide the link to whomever you choose, and they will get the book to read on their preferred device, in their preferred format. BookFunnel is my choice for sharing with each of my books' Advanced Reader Team (if you want to join mine, visit HonoreeCorder.com/ateam).

Host a giveaway.

Amazon has a cool program that allows anyone to give away any book by hosting a giveaway. Amazon Giveaway allows you to run promotional giveaways to create buzz, reward your audience, and attract new followers and customers. You'll find it all the way down on the left side of the page, after the reviews.

Before I share the *how-to's* of the giveaway option, let me offer some advice: I suggest using this option to help other authors. Giving away your own book is, indeed, a fantastic idea and will help you find more readers. But I love the idea of tapping into the karmic forces of the Universe, so why don't you find someone else's book and give it away?

In fact, this book was already completely written and ready for editing when Michael Anderle gave away ten copies of our book *The Prosperous Writer's Guide to Making More Money*. People loved entering the giveaway, Michael had some super fun "you're a loser!" messages for those that didn't win, *and many of the people who didn't win bought the book anyway.* Best of all, Michael made us love him even more (if that was possible) because he paid it forward.

I was inspired by Michael, and I gave away five copies of Chris Syme's book *Sell More Books with Less Social Media*. If you love a book, give it away! By all means, give yours away too. Perhaps you'll find lots of other people will be inspired to share your books with their connections and you can help each other.

Now, let's get to the how-to:

- You start by selecting the book you want to give away; then how many you want to give away. Next, you select your giveaway type (this is where it can get fun, too):
- Sweepstakes. (Winners will be randomly selected after giveaway ends.)
- Random instant win. (Host selects chances of winning, winners are randomly selected.)
- Lucky number instant win. (Host selects "lucky number," winners selected by entry order. You'll select a number between 2-500.)

First-come, first-served. (Host selects number of prizes and everyone wins.)

You have the option to grow your audience by requiring some sort of hoop they must jump through to participate. Here are your choices:

- Follow the author of the book on Amazon
- Follow you (the host) on Twitter
- Tweet a message
- Watch a short video (specifically, an Amazon shorts video)
- Watch a YouTube video
- Answer a poll (my personal favorite, because you get to choose both the winning and losing

messages—this is where your sense of humor can come into play)

Next, you select how long the giveaway will run. You have the option, if you are an Amazon.com seller, to promote the items listed in Seller Central. Your giveaway can be made public or by invitation only. Finally, giveaways are limited to the 50 United States and District of Columbia.

Once you've made all of those decisions, you'll design your Giveaway Page. You'll need:

- A giveaway title
- Your name
- An image of what you're giving away (simple to grab a screen shot of the book)
- Welcome message (for this one and the next two, *have fun* and let your sense of humor come out)
- Win page message
- Lose page message
- Advanced option: allow people to share the giveaway (or not)

Once your giveaway is processed, you'll receive an email confirming the giveaway purchase, and another with the URL to use to share it.

Giveaways are fun, build good karma, and help find readers. I, for one, am going to be hosting them as often as I can! What about you?

Audiobook-specific promotions.

I think audiobooks are the future of books, and you can definitely find more readers with audiobooks. Try these on for size:

- Share clips of your books on social media. Just a few words about your book, along with the image that auto-populates with your link, can spark someone's interest.
- Add your audiobooks to your Goodreads book list (see more, below).
- Audible offers a bounty of $50 for the author who brings new subscribers to their platform. While there are many people who have discovered audiobooks, there are tens of millions of people who haven't. Share your free audiobooks with others, and you'll find listeners for your other books as well.

- Use your promotional audiobook codes to share your book. When you publish on Audible, you get twenty-five free promotional download codes to share as you wish. You can share them through your social media, newsletter, blog, or even a site like Audiobookboom.com.

ADD YOUR BOOK TO YOUR EMAIL SIGNATURE.

You can just add "author" underneath your name (with a link to your Amazon Author Page), or you can add an image of your book cover or covers. You can choose to add a link to your free two-chapter opt-in of your book (see example here – HonoreeCorder.com/YouMustSample), or just link to the site where you sell the most books.

WAIT, YOU DON'T HAVE AN AMAZON AUTHOR PAGE?

I'm always surprised when an author doesn't have an Amazon Author Page. You can get yours at AuthorCentral.Amazon.com. Author Central is where sophisticated readers go to vet a newly-discovered author. It takes just a few minutes to add your professional author photo, a bio that shows your personality, and links to your website and blog. Most important: claim your books in all formats. The minute your book goes live on Amazon, hop over to

Author Central and claim your book. Be sure to check out Dave Chesson's article How to Setup Amazon Author Central and Your Author Page here: https://kindlepreneur.com/amazon-author-central-page/.

And while you're at it … what about Goodreads?

Goodreads is owned by Amazon, however they don't cross-promote when it comes to author information. Goodreads is a rich source of new readers. Here are just a few ways you can use it:

Goodreads is an online social network specifically for authors and readers, with more than twenty-five million members (that's a lot of readers!). Goodreads has just one job: it helps people find the next book they want to read. Think of it as Pandora or Spotify but for books.

Goodreads readers list the books they have read, along with their star rating (and the option to leave a full review). You can also connect with your friends, kind of like on Facebook.

Readers may also vote on lists of their favorite books via Listopia (more on that soon). If someone is curious about the best thriller, they can find a list for it. What is popular in cozy mysteries or naughty fiction? There's a list for it! The more votes a book receives, the higher it ranks on the list.

The best way to learn Goodreads is to sign up (goodreads.com) and explore it *from the reader perspective*. It's free to join, and figuring it out is a lot of fun. You might even discover some delightful new reads for yourself along the way.

Once you've signed up, here are some ways you can use Goodreads for marketing.

Setup your Author Page.

This will take an hour or two, but the investment of time is very worth it. Creating your profile is the first step to connecting with readers, just like you connect with friends on Facebook. Your author page provides statistics about your books and gives readers a place to see what you are up to and what you are reading, again, kind of like Facebook.

Once you have your profile, you can join the Goodreads Author program (https://www.goodreads.com/author/program). The Goodreads Author Program is a free feature designed to help authors reach their target audience of passionate readers. This is the perfect place for new and established authors to promote their books. Just follow the detailed instructions to complete the setup process. Being a Goodreads Author opens the door to the participation of any author in a myriad of Goodreads features. Such as …

Listopia.

The Listopia (https://www.goodreads.com/list) section of Goodreads has a list of any kind of book you can imagine, and adding your books to the appropriate lists can expose you to new readers effortlessly. Simply find the lists appropriate for your books, and then choose the "add books to this list" tab. Use this opportunity to add other books similar to yours to the right lists (this is called good karma and may cause miracles). Then, ask your super fans to vote for your books.

Host a giveaway.

Just like Amazon, Goodreads offers a terrific giveaway option. From your Author Dashboard, you can host a giveaway of your physical or digital books. I've had between 200 to over 700 people enter my giveaways (so far, I've only done physical copies). Goodreads offers giveaway statistics: on average, 750 people enter each Goodreads book giveaway. Of those, 8% will add the book to their to-read list, and 45% of the winners will review the book.

I've done giveaways for seven of my books, eighteen giveaways total. My approach to giveaways is simple: to find someone who wants my book and provide them with a copy. To help ensure they read the book, I write them a handwritten note. In the note, I thank them for requesting my book, tell them I've autographed it, and ask that if they enjoy the book to please leave an honest review. My hope is they will want to read some or all my other books, as well as find information they can use and the inspiration to use it. I like giveaways because they give me one more way to connect with readers.

Volunteer to answer questions.

Two other fantastic features on Goodreads allow you to take questions or host an entire book discussion. The Ask the Author widget allows your readers to ask you questions, as do the Q&A Discussion Groups. Each also allows readers to talk with one another about your book. Both features can help you turn readers who didn't know about your books into fans, and newfound readers into a passionate book enthusiast. Learn more here:

https://www.goodreads.com/author/featured_groups

Connect your blog.

An added bonus of being a Goodreads author is the option to connect your blog directly to your profile. If you are a blogger, add your blog to your Goodreads Author Profile. Those readers just discovering you can learn more about you with little or no extra work on your part. They'll be able to see your latest blog on your Profile, click on it to read more, and even go directly to your personal website.

Ask fans for reviews on Goodreads.

Be sure to ask fans to review your books on Goodreads because it features books solely based on the number of reviews (positive or negative). When you receive an email from a reader telling you how much they love your book, in addition to asking them to leave a review at the online retailer of their choice, be sure to ask them to visit Goodreads as well (and be sure to provide a link to your Author Profile).

Ask for help.

One way to find readers is to ask for help. Post on Facebook, Twitter, or LinkedIn that you need help with: picking the title of a book, choosing between cover designs, what you should write about next, a character name, feedback as an advanced reader, or getting more reviews. Your friends want to help, and if you don't ask, you don't get!

Social Media is a Gateway to Finding Readers

While I am not the social media expert that Chris Syme is, I have learned a thing or two in my thirteen years as an indie author. To complete the picture and become a social media master, you'll want to pick up a copy of *Sell More Books with Less Social Media* and do the free companion course. It is well worth the small monetary investment and substantial time investment.

I break social media into two separate and distinct categories: social and media. I let my assistant handle the majority of my general postings, which include quotes, links to blogs, announcements about my books, or other book business messages. I focus on being social on social media. I stop by each platform once a day (or so) to interact with followers, answer questions, re-post interesting items, share cool discoveries, and connect with new people. Kevin Kruse talks about how to find time to stay on top of the various social media platforms in his book, *Text Me! Snap Me! Ask Me Anything!* He visits social media sites while his coffee is brewing in the morning. I also use "stolen moments" to check social media accounts and interact with others.

Allow me to share with you some effective ways to use social media to find readers:

- **Facebook.** There are three distinct ways you can use Facebook.

  » You most likely have a personal profile on Facebook. You might want to just keep that to friends and family. Or, like me, keeping in mind that nothing on the internet is truly private, open it up to the entire world.

  » You'll also want to create a professional page that highlights you as an author. This is where you'll do the majority of your posting and send the majority of people looking for you on Facebook. It is via your professional page you'll be placing ads if you're so inclined.

  » In addition to the above, savvy Facebookers start communities and invite people to join, creating an alliance of people who, in essence, can become super fans. In addition to my own group, The Prosperous Writers Mastermind, two of my favorites are The Miracle Morning Community and Pat's First Kindle Book. At first you'll be driving every comment, question, post, and discussion. Eventually, the momentum will take over as people feel at home and free to share, ask questions, make posts, and offer thoughts and encouragement to others.

- **LinkedIn.** A fantastic platform for non-fiction authors (not so much for fiction authors, but you can still use some of the advice here), LinkedIn offers several options for finding readers. Increase the likelihood someone will discover your books by doing the following:

  - » Add "author" and the name of your book to your work experience. Also, add your book title(s) to the Publications section and publish your articles and blog posts there as well.
  - » Use a professional headshot. Make sure it's current and you look approachable.
  - » Write your background summary in a conversational tone, and ensure you use keywords related to your book's topic (a.k.a. your expertise).

- **Quora.** I'm new to Quora and haven't quite found my sea legs. But at Kevin's suggestion in the aforementioned book, I hopped on and I'll find a way to include it in my daily repertoire. The reason I mention it here is because if you're a non-fiction author, Quora is quite possibly a place that is being overlooked by other non-fiction authors (just like me, until now).

- **Twitter.** On Twitter, I take Chris Syme's advice and use a pinned tweet to send people to Facebook (where I focus the majority of my social media time). You can customize your header image. Connecting with other authors on Twitter in your genre is a terrific way to make friends. Follow them, share their tweets, and recommend others follow them. Don't be surprised when others begin to do that for you.
- **Instagram.** A picture is worth a thousand *readers.* There are so many terrific ways authors can use Instagram, here are six:

    » **Follow other authors you love.** Comment on their posts, give encouragement, and be a fan.

    » **Follow bloggers who review books.** They just might decide to read and review your book!

    » **Promote your books.** I post the square image used for audiobooks on Instagram because they look so great (smile). You can post a photo on release day, to announce an upcoming release, or to host a giveaway.

  - » **Inspire!** Create your own images using Canva or WordSwag to inspire yourself and your followers. Use your own photo and quotes, or borrow from others (give credit where credit is due, of course).
  - » **Collaborate.** Join with others and use a hashtag (I love #amwriting, #authorlife, and #authorsofinstagram).
  - » **Share.** No need to post naked selfies or share a picture of every single meal you eat. But sharing little slices of life make you real, approachable, and *human.* So share little bits and pieces of your daily life.

- **Pinterest.** I think Pinterest is great, and whenever I need any type of recipe that's where I land. But it's also super for my author business because, just like Instagram, it is so visually oriented. With over 100 million users (and 85% of them female – also known as the gender that reads the most!), you can't ignore this platform, and used well, it can help your discoverability as an author.

  - » **Create a board to showcase your book covers.** You've got great covers and Pinterest is a terrific place to show them off.
  - » **Create a board for your blogs, too.** Whether you're sharing research for your

novel, or additional tips you're discussing in your non-fiction tomes, a separate board for people to follow will increase discoverability.

- **Consider going pro.** You have the option of using a business account, which gives you insight into site analytics (but doesn't change the look of your profile to viewers). In addition, you can build authority and credibility by earning a reputation as the go-to person about a topic. Provide value and inspiration and you'll find yourself with lots of followers who can't wait to read your books.
- **Show your personality in your bio and your pins.** I believe it's our job as authors to simultaneously repel those who don't like us and attract those who do. I believe you can't do the wrong thing with the right person, and vice versa (which I discuss in my TEDx talk, *Authenticity is the New Black:* http://honoreecorder.com/authenticity-is-the-new-black/). As with all social media platforms, being yourself is the best way to find new readers. Give your readers (and future readers) a glimpse of life behind the book.

- **Install the Pin It button on your browser of choice.** Then when you see something interesting, you can pin it to the board(s) of your choosing. Those pins will show up in the timelines of your followers.
- **Ask people to follow you on Pinterest.** You can add the option to follow you on Pinterest to your blogs or email signature. You can make an ask on other social platforms.
- **Size matters.** Figure out the optimal size for your pinned images (http://pinchofyum.com/how-to-hide-an-image-in-a-wordpress-post) because longer pins with words get more re-pins than short images. If you're going to do it, you might as well do it right, right?
- **Be wordy.** You're a writer, so adding a super cool, keyword rich and inviting description of your pin isn't a stretch.
- **Stay at it.** In *The Prosperous Writer's Guide to Making More Money,* my illustrious co-author Brian suggested using a strategy long enough to know whether or not it's working. If you don't get results in 24 hours, don't be tempted to quit. Be consistent, even if you're just pinning one thing a week!

That might not be enough, but you get my gist, right?

» **Be generous and informational.** Follow and re-pin your favorite authors and resources. A single candle can light the world by first lighting other candles. Be an active candle-lighting-candle!

Notes about the above:

Use a consistent profile image so you're immediately recognizable across all platforms.

You might have noticed that some tips (ask people to follow you) apply to all platforms (but you're smart, so I knew I didn't need to repeat myself).

Check your privacy settings regularly. Be sure to use complex passwords so you won't wake up one day to find your account has been hacked. (No faster way to lose readers than to offend them or compromise their social media accounts!)

One other tip: from time to time, ask your readers how they found you. I ask in my different newsletters, in my Facebook group, and in emails I get directly from readers. Keeping track of that data can help you to figure out which of your ninja strategies are *the most ninja of all.*

LESSONS LEARNED

I learned a few lessons from asking readers where they found me, and those were:

1. Never Underestimate the Power of the Ask

Okay, this one is important, so I am repeating it. Look, if you don't a-s-k, you don't g-e-t. It's perfectly fine to get a no, but you always get a no if you don't ask in the first place! I think you'll love the book *Go for No!* by my friends Richard Fenton and Andrea Waltz. It's a good idea to let someone decide for themselves by giving them the option to buy, and along with the ask, to plant the seed that they might want to purchase the books as gifts or even premiums. Premiums are items given en masse, such as at an event in a gift bag. The order of 3,000 books for *Tall Order!* was given to attendees at the company's annual conference, conveniently held in Las Vegas (where I lived at the time). Even if you're a fiction writer, you can still ask the question!

2. Selling Direct has Multiple Advantages

First, you make and keep 100% of the profit. Second, you are a few degrees closer to the reader. *My friend/neighbor/coach wrote this book and you might like it* holds more weight than a book purchased on Amazon with no personal or emotional connection. It will most likely be read sooner, with more enthusiasm, and (I think this is super cool) the reader will lean in the direction of liking the book more than if they had discovered it on their own.

3. Front and Back Matter Can Bring Readers Closer to You

While I didn't know to put a CTA (Call to Action) in the front and back of my book (and oh, how I wish I had!), you can include something for readers to do to connect with you directly, such as download two chapters of one of your other books, or join your mailing list.

One other fantastic ninja idea.

J.A. Huss, who prolifically writes romance books, held a contest and asked her readers to change their Facebook photo to the cover image of her book. J.A. has thousands of fans, so the exposure yielded thousands of additional sales. Imagine having even

20 people change their image to the cover of your book, which their thousands of collective friends and connections would then see. Cool, right?

Brian's two cents on what NOT to do.

Honorée is the best marketing ninja I know. I've learned a bunch from her and I want to reiterate her point about understanding that we spend money and we spend time to make our business grow.

I didn't always think this way. I had to do it wrong to learn.

In 2012, I worked at a phone center and was editing my second novel during breaks. One of the other workers was named Roy Marble. Unless you're from Iowa (or Flint, Michigan) you may not know the name. He's the all-time leading scorer for the University of Iowa men's basketball team and played on the legendary team that went 30–5 in the late eighties. They won their first eighteen games of the season and made it to number one in the nation.

We started talking and he was interested in hearing about my book business. I saw this as a sign he might want a writer to collaborate on a book about him and the Iowa Hawkeye team that did so well.

I was right, and it led to me writing his story about that season. Roy got the university to allow us to launch the book at the Penn State game where 20,000 people would be cheering on their favorite team in Black and Gold. How many authors get a chance to launch like that?

We sold a bunch of books.

It seemed reasonable to keep pushing the sales by setting up some signings. We did a few in Iowa City and other cities close to the university and then reached out to a major grocery store chain. I arranged to have Roy and me do a signing at each of thirty stores in the greater Des Moines area over three weekends.

The grocery store chain included the times and dates for our signing in their email blast and print advertisement the week before we arrived and it did a great job of getting people to come in and meet the author ... okay, nobody wanted to meet me, but they did get a thrill out of meeting Roy.

When all was said and done, we sold around 800 copies. When I got done giving Roy his share, paying for the books, the gas, the food, and everything else. I made just over $200.00

It was an exhausting lesson in ROTI.

There are several things to take away from this story.

1. Getting people to buy from you directly can give one more margin, but it can also lead to greater expenses. So, the margin may not be as good as you think at first.
2. All those sales don't get "recorded" anywhere. They don't improve the ranking of the book on Amazon and this means we don't get additional sales from organic traffic.
3. Doing a book signing is fun … the first couple of times. Then it becomes something you'd rather avoid. The people are nice and it's flattering to scrawl your name across the book, but it doesn't take long before the chit-chat becomes so repetitive that it's hard to keep one's enthusiasm. I was really burned out on signings before we even did the first one in the series of thirty because we had already done five or six others. Yes, it only took five or six for the thrill of the book signing to wear off.

The moral of this story is that one can be a better marketing ninja by deciding NOT to do some things.

One More Ninja Thing

Honorée is even more of a ninja master than she knows. Not only does she come up with these brilliant ideas for marketing, but she also shares them, and has taught me how to think like a marketing assassin.

I've implemented her strategies recently and now it's part of my mindset. I'm constantly on the lookout for opportunities to leave a card or book, and it's got me thinking like a ninja.

Ninja marketing is fun and I want to do more. (I hope you do, too!)

I'm working on adding two pages to each of my print versions and ordering new copies just for leaving in coffee shops and tiny libraries. The page will simply read, "I'm a Travelling Book … When you're done, leave me someplace else (but don't forget to put a comment about where you found me below)" and then have two pages where people can write about how they found the book.

One can imagine a person finding the book and being just as intrigued by where it's been as the actual story. I'm sure the "Travel Pages" will be just as much a hook as the story.

How fun would it be to discover one of your books after it had been roaming around the world for a couple of years? That's my own ninja idea. But it's because Honorée has got me thinking outside the box that I came up with it.

Think Like a Ninja

Honorée again. I love what Brian said about thinking like a ninja, because that is exactly what I have in mind for you, the reader! I didn't originate thinking like a ninja; I learned it from other ninjas who were doing things I hadn't thought of until I heard their ideas. I believe you can take any idea you hear and improve upon it. Claudia Azula Altucher wrote a great book called *Become an Idea Machine*, which you should totally pick up and devour. In her book, she encourages her readers to brainstorm ten new ideas a day. New ideas for anything and everything that's important to you, captured in your journal, can and will spark other ideas. One of them is bound to inspire you or even make you a fortune. Imagine brainstorming ten new book marketing ideas a day, using the ones we've shared in this book? Of course, they won't all be home runs, but if even one of your ideas works wonders, won't you be stoked?

Okay, now that you have a pretty long list of ways to find readers, I'm going to turn it over to Brian, who is going to walk you through some additional lessons he's learned along the way. You'll love not only learning about his journey, but also finding even more gems of inspiration in this next section.

SECTION THREE

CHART YOUR JOURNEY

BRIAN HERE.

I thought I'd take some time to tell you some of the things I've learned along the way. Not everything worked as I had hoped.

When I began, my plan was to build a blog following and then I wanted to bundle my blog posts into a book and sell it. I had been getting a few readers with my snarky woodworking blog that had daily posts chronicling my success and many failures. The reasoning in my mind was that if people enjoyed my humor in little daily posts, they would surely like a collection of those posts.

The first day of blogging happened quite by accident. I came upon a site called Blogger while bored and wrote a post about my foibles in cutting the legs to my workbench. Apparently, measure twice and cut once, which I did, still doesn't get the job done if one is measuring while watching college football.

I had legs of three different lengths and the two that matched were wrong.

After my first blog post, I found a forum on woodworking called Lumberjocks.com. An hour of exploration later and I joined. While setting up the details for my account, I noticed that one could blog on the site. I had already blogged!

Back to Blogger I went. A quick copy and paste later the post was in both places. It felt productive and despite my pure, white-hot hatred of writing, I had enjoyed my little self-mocking rant.

It should be mentioned that this was Jan 2, 2010. I was almost 44 years old and had hated writing since eighth grade. My degree is in economics from Iowa State University. I've yet to take my first writing course.

The mindset on that first day was that I was bored and this little post was simply me entertaining myself. At that point, there wasn't any thought of blogging regularly or one day writing a novel. Those things just never occurred to me.

It's funny how one's perceptions can change with a little (or a lot) of external validation.

On Jan 3, 2010, I woke up and returned to Lumberjocks to read more woodworking stories before heading to the lumberyard to buy more 4x4s to replace the legs I'd made too short. I was shocked.

The little post I'd put up without much thought had been read over 300 times and there were 25 comments. These other woodworkers loved my humor. They told me they had laughed and that my mistakes were ones they'd all made, too, so I shouldn't get discouraged. Mostly they said they wanted more.

I had readers!

The end.

Okay, that wasn't the end. In fact, it turned out to be much harder to convert those readers into book buying customers, or even into blog followers.

At that time in my life, I was living below the poverty line. My parents had let me reside in my grandfather's place, so there was a roof over my head. I had a part-time job doing some social media stuff for a tiny start-up in DC. It was just enough to buy food and pay the utilities.

I was happy, but the thought of making a little extra money was on my mind. So, I wrote another post on Jan 3. I kept writing and getting lots of readers on Lumberjocks. Many of them read every day and left comments.

The plan was to set up my own blog. I figured after a month or so, which would give me time to figure out HOW to set up a blog, I'd tell the Lumberjocks readers and they'd tune in each day.

Well, it didn't work like that. Once I had ExtremelyAverage.com running with daily posts (and the other posts I'd previous written), the folks on Lumberjocks mostly wanted to get my daily updates the way they'd always gotten them before.

My blog numbers were sad.

Eventually, I explained that I was going to only be posting on my blog. Most of the readers didn't follow. I learned that many people are skeptical by nature. They feared that I might be trying to build a business that could make me money. I was doing just that. I like money (and the food that it buys).

Undaunted and knowing I was basically back to square one, I kept at it. When you're at the bottom, there's little reason not to keep going. In fact, Daymond John, the founder and CEO of FUBU, wrote a book called *The Power of Broke*. I just read it and wish it had been around in 2010, because his ideas are sound and motivational. I needed some of that. All I had was a literal hunger for more … pizza and Chinese food.

Something interesting happened as I was writing my blog every day. I was always looking for new and creative ways to craft a post and one day the decision was made to do the post as a chapter of a mystery novel.

I hadn't done any woodworking that day. In fact, all I'd done was buy a Bosch 1.25 HP router. I'd been saving up and talking about it all month on the blog, so the few readers I had knew it was in the cards. A noir mystery starring a detective who liked woodworking and the Brooklyn Dodgers would be perfect.

I named my P.I. Henry Wood.

Henry Wood lived in Brooklyn and had a small agency in Manhattan. In his Brooklyn house, there was a strange closet that occasionally sent him things from the future. He didn't understand it, but liked the last present he'd been given, a Bosch router.

Yes, my detective story had a time travel closet. It was the only way I could figure out to work in the "clue" that I'd finally bought the router. It didn't matter that it was an incongruous thing to have in an historical detective story if one was never going to finish the story.

My readers loved it.

I've written four complete Henry Wood novels and am working on the fifth. There have been more than a few reviews where people sort of shook their head at the closet, but there have also been those who love it. In hindsight, I do think that the silly closet has cost me readers, but that's okay; that closet started me on a path that changed my life.

STAGES OF THE JOURNEY

After a couple of years without much of an idea of where I wanted to go, I realized it was crucial to visualize the signposts on my journey. The following five stages are what I charted out for my book business. The first four might be good for anyone, but the fifth, that's where you'll want to craft your own ultimate destination.

Goals are important. This is something that both Honorée and I agree on 100%. It's best to write them down. I didn't always do that, and I'm sure it slowed my progress, but I did think about them all the time. Now, I keep an Excel file and a notebook where I do write the goals and ideas down.

When I was starting out, I just wanted to make one thousand dollars per month from my writing. If I could do that, it would make my life much easier.

When I quit my day job in late 2015, I had had three months in a row that were all well beyond my goal: $3,000, $7,000, and then $9,800. I left my job and never looked back. There have been a lot of five-figure months since then. Not all of them, though, sometimes sales drop because there's a change in how people react to one's marketing. Then, one needs to regroup and tweak things.

But this is not what we're here to talk about. We want to show people how they build their initial readers and get from zero to one thousand, and once there, where they might want to set their sights.

So, back when my best month ever was $600, I thought about what it had taken to get there and I decided that this mark was Stage One for me.

Stage One

This is when one has only one or two books and if the author isn't telling people about the books, they simply don't sell. It's when the books have fewer than ten reviews.

It's the beginning.

My nature is that I'm an outgoing person who enjoys mingling with others. It isn't hard for me to strike up conversations. I enjoy selling and from a young age found I had a knack for it.

When I was ten, my hockey team in Ames, Iowa, was raising funds. Did we sell cookies? No. We sold the much sexier product, lawn fertilizer. Feel free to insert joke here.

I still remember that the makeup of the fertilizer was 20-10-10, which was supposed to be good. I canvassed the neighborhood and rang every doorbell. Everyone had a lawn and I had a solution to their lawn care needs. Being ten, I think I got most of my sales because I was freaking adorable with my confident pitch.

There was a contest to see who could sell the most bags. I won going away.

The next year, though, it wasn't my pitch that did the job, it was the product because everyone saw great results. I went back and asked for repeat orders and everyone bought again. I thought I was a great salesman. I won the contest a second time.

Sales is about confidence and I probably wasn't a great pitchman at ten or eleven, but the cute of the first year and the repeat sales of the second year gave me a false sense that I was closing the deal. It stuck with me.

Confidence has never been a problem.

So, asking someone for a review, that's about the easiest pitch ever. I truly love my books. No problem, right?

For the first couple of years, I hated it. Asking for a review made my stomach turn. It caused all sorts of stress. It wasn't that I feared a negative review or anything of the sort, it just seemed like the most horrible thing to bother people I liked with and that it would eat up, at the very least, hundreds of hours of their time, probably causing a rift in their marriage, leading to divorce, and lifelong psychological problems for their children. It was quite a burden to carry.

Writing a review takes very little time. Most people are happy to help. The ones that don't want to do it will blow it off. No friendships are harmed in the process and the most important part is that it works.

I had to get over my fear of asking. It's the second most important things one can do when starting out. The first is setting up your mailing list, but we'll talk about that later.

I'm sure there are people out there who never have "review request phobia" and that's awesome. For those of us who do, it's important to ask anyway.

I knew that my fear of failing as an author was greater than the uncomfortable moment when I'd say, *Hey, thanks for letting me know you read my book. Would you mind popping onto Amazon and leaving a review?*

In Stage One we must get reviews, and the focus needs to be on getting to ten. It's harder to go from zero to ten than it is to go from 100 to 200 because of the numbers of sales one needs to get a single review organically. Often it can take one hundred sales to get a single review without asking.

When you've just published your first book, getting to 1,000 sales, so that you can have ten reviews, is almost impossible unless you already have the ten reviews to get people to buy your book. It's a vicious oval. (Circle is so overused in this instance.)

The smaller sites, which are where everyone should start, often require eight to ten reviews, such as Ereader News Today and BKNights.

So, those first ten need to be rounded up. You'll need to beg friends and family. Yes, those reviews will be biased and tend to be five stars.

Finding the Right Readers & Reviewers

Honorée here.

I've put together advanced reader teams for the last dozen or so of my books, as well as for the books in *The Miracle Morning* book series. In addition to my personal experience, I have learned from super secret sources I cannot name here, as well as hearing Bryan Cohen and Jim Kukral (the co-hosts of the Sell More Books Show) and Chris Fox, author of *Six-Figure Author*, as they've talked about how to get reviews. In addition, you don't just want reviews, you want the *right reviews.* Allow me to explain.

Reviews, specifically verified reviews (a review by someone who is confirmed to have purchased the book), left by the avatar for your book help Amazon's algorithms to market the book to other people (lots of other people!). This is done by identifying common characteristics of those who have reviewed the book. With as few as ten reviews, the ideal reader can be identified for your book. Then, Amazon can begin marketing the book aggressively and specifically to others who fit the same profile: those with a high likelihood to buy, read, and love it.

When this step is overlooked or not followed exactly, you miss the short-term and, most importantly, long-term opportunity to have Amazon work on your behalf to promote the book. Most people don't realize this and think any one review is as good as the next or any verified review is a great idea. As you can see, this is not the case.

How do you find them?

If you're a non-fiction author, you should have direct access to your target avatar (ideal reader) because you are an expert in your field. Do your best to find a dozen or more of your clients or connections who have an interest, and ask them to buy (even if you provide a free copy), read, and review your book.

I have, in the past, offered to reimburse readers the cost of the purchase of the book. To date, no-one has taken me up on that offer.

Fiction authors must find readers who already enjoy books in their particular genre. For example, I'm working on a series of thrillers. I'm looking for a few dozen people to read and review my first three books when they are ready. (If this is you, go here to join my fiction Advanced Reader Team at HonoreeCorder.com/HCCorder). I advise you ask anyone and everyone if they read and love the type of books you write. Offer to provide a copy in exchange for an honest review. Because online retailers track the data and profiles of those who leave reviews, it won't be long before they will be marketing your book to people you might not otherwise be able to reach—just because they share a similar love of your type of book.

Make sense? Okay, I'll pass the baton back to Brian.

Brian again.

Yes, most readers will know that a book with only a handful of reviews isn't really a 4.9 average. Those readers will still be willing to click on "Look Inside" and perhaps it will be worth their while.

One of the key elements in driving sales is running promotions where one gives one's book away for free or puts it on sale for ninety-nine cents. Honorée talked about this some and she's right. There are many venues that will accept your ads, but the best ones have guidelines in regard to the number of reviews the book must have before it's eligible for promotion.

This is especially true of books that are free or ninety-nine cents.

In Stage One you want to go after every review you can imagine.

A word of caution, though, is don't try to game the system with fake reviews. Amazon, in particular, is clever. They will catch those reviews and hit the delete button. In fact, there have been so many people trying to cheat that Amazon tends to err on the side of delete. This may one day cause a legitimate review to disappear and that can be frustrating. Don't blame Amazon, blame the authors who are trying to take a shortcut.

Please remember that it takes years of hard work to become an overnight success. (Honorée's note: Amen.) Also, if writing is something you enjoy, then worrying about how quickly you make it to your goal is silly. You're having fun along the way and when the day comes that you can do it full-time (if that's your goal), it will be a nice moment, but it isn't the only goal. First and foremost, writing should be about exploring what you can do as a writer and taking pride in the progress that comes with the journey.

The short version is this …

1. Ask people to review your book.
2. Always be asking so that it is part of your routine. That means that if someone asks about your book, you tell them, and they say they may check it out, go ahead and ask them if they could please write a review afterward. Do it even if you think they are just being nice. Who knows, they may buy your book and do exactly as they said.
3. Use the smaller sites that don't require eight to ten reviews to run promotions. Any time you get your book into someone's hands, you've done a good thing for your business.
4. Be honest (leave the cheating for the cheaters). Work hard and you'll find it's worth it.

Stage Two

There is one site that is better than all the rest. It's called BookBub and that's where you want to advertise your book.

Sounds easy, right?

No.

Everyone wants to advertise their books on BookBub because the results are amazing, but there are a limited number of slots available each day, so placement is competitive. I've had free promotions that included a BookBub promotion and the difference between them and other venues can be 40,000 downloads versus 3,000.

In every promotion I've had through them, currently at thirteen, my ROI (return on investment) has been at least 500% and usually an additional 50–130 reviews.

The more reviews your book has, the better the chance someone will buy it. Of course, there are some people who don't care about review totals. Maybe you're one of those people. Maybe you think the reviews are all biased. You are not representative of the reading population.

If you can remind yourself daily, *I am not my reader*, it will serve you well. One mistake I've made repeatedly is that without any data to support my decisions, I assume the way I think about books is universal (or at the very least in the majority).

This is dangerous because it can cause one to miss countless opportunities.

The biggest example in my life of how this type of thinking has cost me thousands of dollars is the idea (in my mind) that nobody reads paper books anymore. I read 98% of the books I buy on my iPad or iPhone, so I assume everyone does the same. This idea was so strong in my mind that I've not bothered to make print versions available for most of my books. Even now, only half of them have print versions, which is something I'm working on fixing.

You know what happened when I started putting up my print books for sale? Some people bought them. My Kindle sales are still the biggest part of my monthly revenue, but the percentage is shifting. Six months ago, when I only had two of twelve titles in print, less than one tenth of one percent of my sales were print.

I used this ridiculous statistic to justify *not* putting my books into InDesign and getting the layout done so I could sell the print versions. *Print just doesn't sell for fiction,* my voice would say.

The little voice in my head should have been yelling, *How do you know?! You don't even give readers the chance to buy the paper version.*

Even after people would email me asking when the paperback would be available, I still resisted.

My last month revenue saw print making up 2.3%, which was up from the month before and has grown every month over the last few since I started making them available. I spend a ton of money on advertising and now the people that prefer the print version have that as an option.

This is why we don't assume we are our reader. I've left thousands, perhaps tens of thousands of dollars on the table over the last few years. What's worse, and this is nearly unforgivable, I've left potential avid fans on the table.

This book is about finding your true fans because they're the key to success. They're the ones who will buy everything you put out. If you get enough of these fine folks, you'll be able to do this for a living.

So, back to my point about the importance of reviews. If we think like a statistician, then we need to consider the entire book-buying population. If there is a pool of, say, ten million readers, we know that some of them read mystery books. Let's say we're talking about four million people. Of those people, their buying habits will vary. Some will buy only e-books, others will only check out books from the library, others prefer print, while some want used books bought in cozy indie bookstores with cats on staff.

This means that the reasons one buys a book can be just as varied. Some people will judge a book by its cover. Others will read the description and that will be the key to their decisions. Some will use the "Look Inside" feature and go from there. A portion will begin with the number of reviews and the rating. I would wager that every person has a habit they stick to. In each case, there will be a first step.

If that first step is deciding if the cover is appealing, then you'd better have a good cover. If it is social proof, then you better have reviews.

All of this is to say that the monetary ROI is only part of the picture, and getting a bunch more reviews from a BookBub promotion is more valuable than you may imagine.

Stage Two involves getting enough reviews to give yourself the best chance of being chosen for one of those coveted BookBub slots. They are picky. In their rejection notice, which most people will get on their first try, the email states that they reject 80% of the submissions. (Note: Not my wonderful co-author, Honorée, though. She was one for one out the gate.)

The reasons for rejections are many. Poor cover design, weak book descriptions on the sales pages of the various sites (such as Amazon, Barnes & Noble, Kobo, Apple iBooks, and Google Play), and just sheer volume of submissions can all play a part.

We know from statements made publicly by BookBub representatives that they don't have a specific minimum guideline for number of reviews, but they have said that they like to see fifty.

Yes, the big Five-Oh is your goal for Stage Two. You want to get your first BookBub ad and add a bunch of juice to your sales.

There's one other aspect of the BookBub promotions that is probably the most valuable over the lifetime of your career. It's that you pick up extra subscribers to your mailing list. Again, we'll talk about that later.

So, you've managed to get to ten reviews in Stage One. Now, in Stage Two, you're still thinking about garnering reviews while you work on your next book. The venues that require eight to ten reviews are available and you're using them to promote your book.

Run promotions and keep at it until you hit fifty.

It doesn't hurt to start submitting to BookBub in Stage Two. You may sneak in with fewer than fifty and that will launch you into Stage Three. Just be prepared. Each rejection stings a little. It's the same with one-star reviews. You'll need to build a coping mechanism for those tiny gut punches. We all go through it. In fact, pick one of your favorite authors and go read her one-star reviews.

Stage Three

For me I felt I'd reached a third stage when I was consistently getting BookBub advertisements at a pace of four or five per year. Once I knew what it took and that no matter how cool I thought I was, I would still get rejected most of the time, I stopped worrying about it.

One trick I found that has worked for me is to put in for an ad at ninety-nine cents and then if it gets rejected, immediately come back with a request for a

FREE promotion. This strategy helped me get more BookBub ads and improved my bottom line.

Most of my ads have been for FREE promotions and the results are always profitable and help build readership.

Realizing that I would need to do more than just BookBub ads to continue the growth, I started looking to venues like Facebook, Instagram, and Amazon for advertising.

These methods of advertising are more of a challenge. One needs to do a fair amount of study to figure out what works.

I started out by taking a course on Facebook Ads and it failed for me. The course was well-designed and I liked the teachers. The information was helpful because I learned enough to be able to place ads, but their target audience was people who were selling much larger ticket items like consulting. At the end of the course, the teacher even said he didn't know how one could use Facebook for selling books because the margin was so small.

The next one I took was Mark Dawson's Facebook Advertising for Authors Course. It's designed for authors and made all the difference in the world. Still, it's a great challenge to do profitably and you will need to understand that most of the things you try will fail. You must test and test and test to find a plan that works. It requires a lot of time and patience.

I've had similar experiences with all the places I've looked into advertising on a cost-per-click basis. Each one has challenges.

The upside is that once you crack one of these platforms, your revenue goes up substantially. Depending upon the month, I might spend $2,000–$4,000 on advertising and will typically get an ROI of 100%–300%.

Please understand that ROI isn't the only important measure, and sometimes I'd rather have lower ROI with a higher actual profit left over at the end of the month. As an example, I had two months last year where the ROI was vastly different, but the lower one was preferable.

In Month One I spent $4,000 on ads, and in Month Two I spent $700.

In Month One, I had a profit of $7,800, while my Month Two profit was only $5,300. So while my ROI for Month Two was the greatest (757%), it was actually Month One where I made the most money, even though my ROI was much less (195%).

One might ask the question, "Why didn't you spend the $4,000 in Month Two and really crush it?"

I would have if it had been possible. The hardest part about the various advertising platforms is figuring out how and when to scale. Some months the clicks are cheap, while others they are expensive. I spend as much as I can and keep an eye on which ads are performing well.

In the case of the second month, I had a couple ads that were crushing it. I tried to create similar ads to scale up the spend, but those ads just didn't do well.

In the first month, I had lots of ads performing reasonably well and could spend a lot more money, even though it was at a lower ROI.

The point is to have as much money left over at the end of the month. This profit or throughput is the ultimate goal, so some advertising decisions require looking at the big picture and making the decisions accordingly. If I had tried to spend $4,000 in the second month, most of those ads would have lost money and I wouldn't have been left with $5,300. It would have been much less.

In this stage, which is where I consider myself now, one can expect a lot of months with five-figure sales (summer months can be a challenge). The more of those months one has, the larger one's reader base becomes.

To do well in this business, you'll need to keep writing and producing new work or eventually the sales will dry up. The further through each stage you get, the longer the tail becomes on how quickly sales drop when you take a break.

In my above ROI example, a portion of those sales would have happened regardless. In my internal calculations, I factor in the read through and existing reader base to get a less inflated number.

To better understand how much of my revenue was being driven from ad sales, I took the month of July 2016 off from running ads. When I last did this in 2013, my sales went from $400-600 a month down to $150.

This time the sales dropped to $3,000. I then ramped up my advertising again and was able to get back to five-figures almost immediately. I know it seems crazy to give up so much revenue, but I truly value the data. Also, the month of July was such that I didn't really have the time to manage my ads like I typically would, so it was a perfect time for a test.

This example is just to reinforce the power of working your way through the stages. I'm confident that my sales will continue be enough to support being a full-time author even through dry spells of writing. It means that if I want to take a vacation, I don't stress out about it. Even a break can be profitable if it gets one's writing juices replenished.

Stage Four

It's important to remember that my five stages are simply a construct I've created to allow me to keep focused. It may be wise to plan your own stages based upon your objectives. I'm sure it would serve you better than simply adopting mine, but I hope it gives you a sense for the theme of stages.

I've been a full-time author for over a year. Financially, I'm doing better than I have ever done before, so it begs the question, why even have other stages?

I don't *need* to make more money. I do have a burning desire to pursue other projects and dreams, though. I keep a journal of ideas that I'd like to go after. They range from wanting to buy a manufacturing company, to starting an alternative energy company, to inventing new technology that improves upon existing tech. I dream big.

Most of these ideas will require money. So, to continue to grow and explore my passions, I give you Stage Four.

This is the point where I focus on building a strong enough list to be able to launch books onto *The New York Times Best Sellers* list.

I've never been on *The New York Times* or *USA Today* lists. I'm less interested in the moniker "*The New York Times* bestselling author or *USA Today* bestselling author" than I am cracking the math behind doing it on a consistent basis. It isn't complex. Just grow a big list of avid readers.

Let's assume that most weeks one can crack the *USA Today* list for fiction with 10,000 sales in a week (usually, I have 2,000–3,000 sales over an entire month). It's a big number to be sure.

Working the math backward, let's start with 10,000 and divide that by point two. Go ahead and punch that into the calculator on your phone. It gives you the number 50,000. That's the number of people that need to open your email blast at a rate of 20% click through, to get the 10,000 people to your page for the new book.

But it's not that simple. Not all of those people will buy it.

So, let's say we know that 1 in 3 of your fans who click will buy it, then you need 150,000 people to open your email.

How many people on an email list would it take to get 150,000 to open it?

I've talked with many authors and most of them find that 50–60% open rate is reasonable. This is *much* better than the industry standard for newsletters, which is 12.5%. And the click through rate for authors is typically 20–22%.

That means that a 300,000 people list would probably do the trick. It may be a smaller number depending upon how one manages one's list. If one sends regular messages, that could mean a higher open average. If one has a series where people are dying for the next installment, it may not require a list of even half that size.

There are lots of variables, but that's what Stage Four is all about. Building the list, testing the results, trying to improve the results, and then using it as a tool to achieve one's goals.

Another factor with my example of trying to launch on a list is that one may also be doing targeted ads or have run a quality pre-order campaign.

All the sales during the time your book is up for pre-order count in that first week. So, if you can convince 2,000 people to pre-order, then the target is easier to hit.

The point is that a mailing list of substantial size can vault your titles into a whole other level of exposure. Getting enough sales in one week to make a list will also land your book near the top of Amazon's Overall Top Seller list, which is more exposure.

Perhaps your list is only good enough to get you 7,000 sales, but you get them all on a Monday or Tuesday and the book is on page one of the Top 100 for a couple of days and is #1 across your sub categories. That will yield more sales.

For me, this stage is all about scaling up in a much bigger way than I've done through Stage Three.

Stage Five

I'll be the first to admit that when I first imagined Stage Five, it was the sort of dream that one puts out there, a seemingly unachievable goal. It still feels that way, but I find value in having it there, waiting for me. Perhaps when I get deep into Stage Four, I can give it some serious thought.

My Stage Five is selling one of my novels as a movie. I had imagined that I'd write a screenplay for *Killing Hemingway* and I still might, but I've since learned that most studios prefer that the author *not* write the screenplay. They would rather have an A-List Screenwriter, A-List Producer, and A-List Director so that if it goes poorly, they don't get blamed since they had all the right people. I get that.

Still, I would like to learn the craft of screenplay writing, so I may use *Killing Hemingway* to try it out.

My Stage Five is unlikely to be anyone else's Stage Five, especially if you are a non-fiction writer, but that's okay. It's a great idea to make your own stages (or at the very least, this last one).

When the day comes that I have achieved this goal, I'll likely create five more stages to help guide me from that point in my life. What's important is to have a plan, something you can visualize daily, which will help as a guide through decision making. Each day your hours are limited and right now you're focused on gaining readers. Once you get good at picking up some loyal fans, you don't want to get stagnant; that's why having a few milestones well off in the distance will keep you from periods of being unproductive.

Growing Your Mailing List

Not growing my mailing list is something I did horribly wrong for the first few years of my business. I'm just now understanding the power of the list and where I went wrong.

When I began, I had my blog and people could subscribe. Every time another author would give advice about the importance of "your list," I thought that they meant my list of subscribers. A strong blog subscriber list is a wonderful thing but it is *not* the same as an author list. People who enjoy daily posts of 500–1,000 words may not be interested in your books. They may not want to hear about your new release. Of course, you'll certainly mention the new tome on the blog and it will drive some sales, but it isn't the same as a dedicated list.

The author newsletter is an important tool. And there are things you must understand about it to fully appreciate the necessity of dedicating time to the building of such a list.

As I mentioned above but is worth repeating, the following three points are crucial to know.

1. Never call it a newsletter. I suggest, instead, calling it an "author reader group."
2. Typical newsletters have an open rate of 12.5%. Author reader groups open their emails at a rate of 50–60%.
3. CTR (click-thru rates) for newsletters is 1–2%, while author reader groups click through 20% of the time.
4. The reason one never calls their newsletter a newsletter is because that term has been beaten to death and people are tired of getting newsletters. Avid readers, however, love hearing from their favorite authors. Being part of a reader group seems much less intrusive.

I learned this from Nick Stephenson and Mark Dawson, both of whom tested landing page copy using "newsletter" versus "reader group" and the results were clear. I've also done my own tests and my results were similar to what they had found. People are 50% more likely to sign up for your list if it is a reader group than if they're asked to subscribe to a newsletter.

There may come a day where "reader group" is beaten to death and at that point we'll need to come up with another idea, but until then, use READER GROUP.

The reason it's handy to remember the open and click-thru rates is that those benchmarks will aid in guiding you as you write your emails that go out to the readers.

Style and Copy Matter

When I worked as a data analyst in the marketing department at a major insurance company, I learned that they always tested their advertising mailing envelopes to see which design performed the best. The control group would be a plain white envelope and there would usually be four to six designs created by the art department. It is interesting to note that during my five years in that department, the control group (blank white) never lost. At the time, I believe it was undefeated. For some reason, those blank envelopes were opened more often (we surmised the open rate because the material inside was the same across all the envelopes and included unique telephone numbers that allowed tracking) but that didn't stop the art department from continuing to look for a way to improve.

Remember this story when you're testing your own emails. Try some fancy ones with lots of pretty pictures and designs for part of your list. Then do a plain "get to the point" email with minimal design and see which one wins.

(Honorée here: I've tried fancy and simple. Simple wins every time.)

You'll learn a lot about your audience that way.

It isn't just the design you should test. My own experience has been that the copywriting is incredibly important. In fact, I'd recommend taking the time to read a book or two on the subject (*The AdWeek Copywriting Handbook: The Ultimate Guide to Writing Powerful Advertising and Marketing Copy from One of America's Top Copywriters* by Joseph Sugarman is my favorite). Copywriting is an art form. This is especially true in emails.

You're not just picking the right words, you're also making decisions regarding the length of paragraphs. Hint: Short and sweet is the way to go.

It was hard for me to switch gears from writing prose to writing copy. For a long time, I assumed that because my readers liked my writing style, I should stick to that for my emails. I assumed incorrectly. My readers want the facts.

They want me to get to the point.

Do some tests and find out what your readers want.

Not to dwell on the whole "read some ad copy books" thing, but once I understood the goals and methods of great copywriters, it changed how I created my ads. More importantly, it changed how I viewed the description I wrote for the books on my Amazon pages.

Before reading about ad copy, there were few things in the world I hated more than writing that 200–300 word description. Those things were peas, fruit in Jell-O, and my inability to dunk (I'm short).

Once I had learned a few tips and tricks, I tried reworking my book descriptions and found that the next day my sales conversions went up. I was running the same number of ads. They were getting the typical number of clicks but those clicks were resulting in more paid sales and KU downloads (as judged by a spike the following day in page reads)

Having copywriting skills will help with your reader group emails, your description, and the way you write when trying to persuade someone that you're the right person for the job. Let me explain the last one.

There's a great thing called HARO, which stands for Help a Reporter Out. It's a three-time daily email blast that all authors should subscribe to because of the opportunities it can provide. Each email contains calls for experts in various areas to be interviewed for articles, blogs, and podcasts. The reporters put out these calls and then people write them back. If your response piques their interest, it may lead to your story getting included in their article or them asking you to be interviewed for a podcast or show.

For the first two years I subscribed, I didn't have a single one of my responses hit the mark. Once I started using what I'd learned about copywriting, I was able to craft emails that kept the reporter reading. That's the key. The first line needs to be short and intriguing enough that they want to read the second line. It's about moving the reader through your message all the way until the end.

When I get to the end, then I bust out my author skills and create a cliff hanger sort of call to action. The action being, "If you want to hear the rest of the story, I'd be happy to talk to you."

It isn't just blogs, podcasts, and newspapers that are looking for people to interview. I just opened the HARO from last night and Fox News Network, Online Wall Street Journal, CNBC, and the Associated Press (AP) all were searching for experts. It takes only a couple of minutes per day to scan the request emails and see if there's anything with which you might be able to help.

Here's an example of one I wrote to a podcast looking for marketing people who had overcome a PR nightmare.

> Dear Rob (not his real name),
>
> I'm a full-time author who almost destroyed my career with one tiny blunder at 3:00 a.m.
>
> In the world of indie publishing (and now traditional, too) the most coveted advertising spot is a listing in the daily email blasts of BookBub. They are the king makers.
>
> I had secured a spot for the fourth mystery in my *Henry Wood Detective* series, *Edge of Understanding*, and was so thrilled I couldn't sleep the night before the promotion. It would become the best day of my life ... for ten minutes before disaster struck.
>
> Typically, a BookBub ad will also give a small boost to an author's other books. *Henry Wood: Edge of Understanding* was going to be FREE for two days. I'd had other similar promotions for the first three books in the series and each time they had risen to the #3 spot on the overall Top 100 Amazon free rankings. This was the highest rated of my four books with 4.6/5 stars on 50+ reviews and it was my best cover.

This would be the time I finally made it to number one!

The email blast went out at 10:00 a.m. and the downloads started pouring in at a rate of around 190 per minute for the first hour. I was refreshing my report page so fast there was a risk of serious finger injury.

When four o'clock rolled around, I checked and my book had hit #1. I was so excited I literally jumped around a bit. It was a goal reached and I couldn't be more thrilled.

Ten minutes later there was a new review. One-star. The person was not happy with the book they received. I shrugged. It happens. A few minutes later there was another one-star review and the person was complaining that *Henry Wood* wasn't even in book four.

What?

I went to Amazon and checked the "Look Inside."

My heart sank. The world stopped turning for a moment. I knew what had happened.

My satire, *Underwood, Scotch, and Wry*, had just been released. At 3:00 a.m. I received an email with the mention of a single typo that had been found. The beauty of being both author and publisher was that it took me only a few seconds to fix and then to recompile it.

The problem was that I was tired. I got onto my dashboard and uploaded the fixed version of *Underwood, Scotch, and Wry* but not over the old version. I uploaded over *Edge of Understanding.*

At the point where I realized what I had done, 40,000 copies of the WRONG book had been sent out. People were pissed. They were leaving one-star reviews at an alarming pace.

There were tears as I sat at my desk watching my best book's review rating plummet to 3.2. My first thought was that I'd destroyed one of my novels that I'd worked so hard on. At the time, it was a big chunk of my monthly revenue, too, so that made it even more dire.

And my #1 ranking was now a source of pain not joy.

If you'd like to hear the rest of the story and learn how I turned the worst day of my life into a positive, please let me know.

Sincerely,

Brian D Meeks (Sometimes Arthur Byrne)

Let's look at that email. I started with a hook. In most copy, I try to keep the hook short because the reader may not give it a chance if it looks too long, but I figured Rob was seeking people to interview for his podcast, so he would at least read the first sentence.

In the first sentence, I told him what I do and hinted at a disaster that I had to overcome. There was also a bit of a hook in the time of 3:00 a.m. It adds a bit of mystery.

What could I possibly have been doing at that hour that could ruin my career?

Then I went into storytelling mode and laid out the details of my horrible blunder.

I finish the story, talking about how much pain it caused me to think about reaching number one. I've told this story to people enough (and it's 100% true) to know that by the time I get to the end, they feel sick for me. Some probably feel almost as bad as I did at the time. Most people can remember a time they did something completely by accident and messed something up. It resonates.

But here is where my understanding of copywriting paid off. I didn't tell Rob what I did next. In the beginning, I hint at the fact that the blunder only "almost" destroyed my career.

I finish with a call to action. If Rob wants to hear the happy ending to the story, he'll have to reach out to me and continue the conversation.

He did just that and I was interviewed for his podcast. It went extremely well.

Get More Conversions

Now that you're convinced of the importance of building your reader group, you need to understand the importance of what Nick Stephenson describes as "reader magnets" in his excellent book: *Reader Magnets: Build Your Author Platform and Sell more Books on Kindle*. In short, a reader magnet is something of value that you give away to help close the deal on the potential reader signing up for your reader group. Honorée sometimes uses the first two chapters of her books, other times she gives away valuable resources useful to her readers.

The most common way to do this in fiction is to give away the first book of a series. I do this for my mystery, science fiction, and satire series. I know that if I can get people to take the first book in these series that they are more than likely to buy the next book and possibly continue reading until the end of the series. Furthermore, some of those readers will enjoy my writing enough that they will jump to another one of my series.

The beauty of the age in which we live is that our books are a zero-raw material product. Each Kindle novel or work of non-fiction is, at its core, just a series of ones and zeros that is supported by a tiny bit of electricity.

Imagine how expensive it would be to build a list giving away a print version of your book? You have not only the cost of printing it but the shipping, too.

All of this sounds great unless you're just beginning.

Maybe you only have one book and are feeling frustrated that my advice doesn't apply to you. Well, we all had only one book once upon a time.

What I did for my reader magnet for a long time was I wrote a 7,700-word short story that was a standalone thriller. It was different from my mystery book, but it was a bit more of Brian Meeks writing that I thought readers might enjoy. The hope was if they enjoyed *Henry Wood Detective Agency*, they would be interested in the short thriller.

I had it edited and created a cover. I wrote on the cover that it was a 30-minute thriller, so they would know this wasn't a full-blown novel. It's important to set expectations. I didn't want anyone to be upset at the length.

Yes, even something that's free can still piss people off if they're disappointed because it didn't meet expectations.

So, the things you'll need to consider when setting up your reader magnet is the details in making the whole system work.

It starts with a link in the front and back matter of your book telling the reader of the offer. That link needs to go somewhere. I have landing pages for each of my three different lists.

A moment of discussion about the landing pages. It's important that those pages not have any other links or buttons that might distract your potential subscriber. That means there aren't links back to the beginning of your blog. It also means that putting in links to other books you may have written is also a bad idea. If they want more books by you, they've got the links in the book they just read. At this point you want them to subscribe. That's goal number one.

You're giving them two options. Click on the button Join My Reader Group (remember: *never* "subscribe to my Newsletter") or click to close the browser.

Once they click a box comes up that asks for their email address: *Where would you like me to email your copy of (title of the book)?*

It's important to understand that people don't like to give out their email addresses. If you have a box asking for the email address on the first page it will cause some resistance. If the potential subscriber has just taken an action like clicking on the button, they've passed the point of committing. Now, you're just trying to do as they wish, but you still need to know where to send it. At this point, in their mind it is only logical that the email address would be required and their reticence is gone.

What happens next is interesting. The pop up box where they entered the email address is something created by the email service you use. Many people like MailChimp, I use ActiveCampaign (Honorée uses and loves AWeber), which is more expensive but has some nice features.

I began with MailChimp, though, and they have made it easy to setup your mailing list, which also includes the code you'll need to create the little box for gathering the email.

Imagine you've built a nice landing page that had enticing ad copy based upon what you learned from reading Sugarman's *AdWeek* book. You've called the button Join Your Book Title's Reader Group, and the email capture form comes up after that. How does the book get to the reader?

That's the question that stumped me for a while. What I did starting out was to include a link to a Dropbox folder that had the MOBI (Kindle), EPUB (other digital platforms), and PDF versions of the book that readers could then download. That works just fine, but now there's a better way. It's called BookFunnel and Honorée mentioned it earlier. This is a service that delivers your book for you and it's wonderful. I use BookFunnel now.

There is only one more thing about your list. It's crucial that you understand the importance of keeping in touch with your readers. Remember, they like your writing and want to know what's going on. This is an area where I've dropped the ball and I can tell you from experience that some people will forget who you are if you don't remind them from time to time. They may have signed up because of the reader magnet, they may have even enjoyed the free book you sent them, but if it is six months before they hear a peep out of you, they'll have forgotten who you are and won't be as inclined to take an action, such as buy your new book.

It can be hard to get over the feeling you're being annoying, but most people won't be bothered by updates if they're not more than once or twice per month. Doing this will keep your list fresh.

When you're comfortable with all of this list stuff, you can start to consider building an auto-responder campaign that helps during the early stages of having a new subscriber. It's basically a series of evergreen emails that would be of interest to the new subscriber, that keeps you in their mind.

The Long Game

When one is beginning, the focus is on adding readers one at a time. That's normal and there's value in doing that hard work. It's a time where we get over any insecurity we might have about asking someone to try our book. This is when we learn that asking someone if they would like to give our book a read isn't such a big deal.

Back when I had only one book out, I spent a lot of time on Twitter. I wasn't there because I thought it would sell a ton of books, I was there because (in those days) people would just hang out and talk about things. I'd have conversations with my Twitter friend in Malaysia about Liverpool F.C. There would be chats with the guinea pig, BiggusPiggus, about the travel business run by his humans. I follow a lot of guinea pigs! There would be discussions with bloggers about how to build our audience. It wasn't about always selling.

One day a woman that I had barely talked to, tweeted out, "I've just finished a book and need something new to read. Any suggestions?"

> At this point, I was still a little shy about asking, so I eased into it. "What type of genres do you like to read?"
>
> "I like everything."

"Do you like mysteries?" I asked, hopefully.

"I love mysteries."

"I've written a mystery called the *Henry Wood Detective Agency*. Would you like a link so you could check it out?"

"Yes, please."

I zipped over to Amazon, got the link, and then tweeted it back to her. About five minutes later, I got a tweet back. It read, "I've bought your book and read the first chapter. I love it!"

That's one sale. It's not a big deal, but at the time it was huge. Back then I had many days without sales so each one was treasured. That wasn't the amazing part, though. It was the moment that I realized that we (authors) live in the most incredible time to be publishing our stories.

In a span of less than ten minutes, from my computer in Martelle, Iowa (pop. 252), I made a sales pitch, closed the deal, *and* had the product delivered to the customer—who lived in Antigua. If that same conversation had been between Samuel E. Clemens (Mark Twain) and a woman in Antigua, it would have been by mail. It would have taken months for the back and forth and then still more time to deliver the book.

This realization made me feel unstoppable. Anything was possible. All I needed to do was continue to work and I'd figure out ways to get my books in the hands of readers.

And, all you need to do is continue to work, continue to write, and discover even more ways to get *your* books in the hands of readers!

The Time Has Come

Honorée here.

The purpose of this book is not just to give you a whole bunch of ideas. The purpose of this book is to give you a whole bunch of ideas that you use, ideas that create a spark and birth other ideas—all of which you deploy with great success. If Brian and I have done our job well, we've inspired you with our ideas and our ideas have done a Vulcan mind-meld with some of your ideas, spawning new and even better ideas. Hopefully, you have been inspired and have already started penciling in some ninja secrets that will cause us to exclaim, *That is genius!*

The best part about ideas is that once they start coming, they come fast and furious. They won't all be gold-star gems of brilliance, and that's okay. Because you've taken the time to add intention and purpose to your direction, you'll most likely be able to sort through our ideas and the ones you have, then you can choose the best ones for you to use right now.

I have shared with you my favorites, and now I'm putting on my coaching hat with the goal of getting you into action. So, before you read any further, grab a pen and some paper, your Bullet Journal, or start a new Evernote document, and together let's craft a finding readers plan for you.

I want you to find and attract new readers as soon as tomorrow, or even today! So let's hurry up and get your plan in place, identify the ninja ideas you think will work best, and get you on the road to finding more readers fast.

When you're ready, turn the page …

SECTION FOUR

YOUR ACTION PLAN

HONORÉE HERE.

Now that you've identified what you want from your writing, you can get down to the business of creating your very own action plan, which you can populate with your numbers and intended action items.

I've used big numbers in this plan on purpose—because I'm a big thinker and I believe in abundance. If at any time the numbers seem too big or overwhelming, *simply change them*. You may not want to do anything more than make enough to be a full-time writer, and that's fantastic. Doing what you love isn't all about the money; it's mostly about being able to make enough money to do what you love. Your first Action Plan could be to make $1,000 a month, instead of $10,000, so you'll just divide all of the numbers by 10. Start where you are, make incremental increases as desired, rinse and repeat. Fair enough? Keep this in mind: in 2008, I made $28.00 on Kindle (thank you, GetBookReport.com!). Everyone starts somewhere, so just begin where you are, and take it from there.

On the flip side, perhaps you are among those who have already made $10,000 a month and are looking to go to your next level. Good for you! This action plan works just as well for scaling up, regardless of the intended size of your business or income.

Your Action Plan

I've provided an example to get you started:

2017 ACTION PLAN EXAMPLE

What I want from my writing: *I am a full-time prosperous author earning in excess of $10,000 per month from my writing.*

Goal #1: $120,000 2016 income = $10,000 per month

Goal #2: 95 total e-books sold per day

Action Items:

1. Do one podcast interview every three days (122 total)
2. Add 5000 people to my author email list (13.69 per day)
3. Update opt-in
4. Revise *Autoresponder Madness* sequence
5. Have twice daily updates in private FB group
6. Post on personal timeline 4x/week
7. One blog post per week
8. Read top 100 other books in my genre, write reviews on Amazon/Goodreads
9. Leave postcards in various locations (elevators, bookstores, etc.)
10. Write 2000 wpd in current WIP to keep with my schedule (730,000 words)

You can download a blank version here: HonoreeCorder.com/FindingReaders.

Go Get 'em, Writer!

Brian and I sincerely hope you take the time to create your Action Plan. Mostly, we want you to execute it! Many an awesome plan has collected dust instead of coming to life, and in your case, that would be tragic! We know that because you not only bought this book, you took the time (your most precious resource) to read it, and probably have started, if not finished, your own Action Plan.

Just as we want you to create and execute your plan, we want your words to find life and the readers who will love them. We encourage you to shed any limiting beliefs that stand in your way, tune into (and turn up!) the inner voice that is cheering you on, and go for it 100%.

Prosperity for Writers, both the book and the course, can help you to eliminate any beliefs you have that aren't serving you (you'll find links in the Resources Section at the back of this book for both, as well as all of our other books).

The only thing standing between you and the readers who will be delighted to find you is, well, not a thing. Rock on, and be sure to write us and let us know how it's going!

Resources

LINKS TO OTHER BOOKS IN THE PROSPEROUS WRITER SERIES:

Prosperity for Writers: A Writer's Guide to Creating Abundance
(The Prosperous Writer Series Book 1)
http://tinyurl.com/ProsperityforWriters

Prosperity for Writers Productivity Journal: A Writer's Workbook for Creating Abundance
http://tinyurl.com/P4WJournal

The Nifty 15: Write Your Book in Just 15 Minutes a Day
(The Prosperous Writer Series Book 2)
http://tinyurl.com/Nifty15

The Prosperous Writer's Guide to Making More Money: Habits, Strategies, and Tactics for Making a Living as a Writer
(The Prosperous Writer Series Book 3)
http://tinyurl.com/AuthorMoney3

LINKS TO OUR READER GROUPS & OTHER AWESOMESAUCENESS:

The Prosperous Writer Mastermind:
HonoreeCorder.com/Writers

***The Prosperous Writer's Guide to Finding Readers* Bonuses:**
HonoreeCorder.com/FindingReaders

BEST BOOK BUSINESS READS:

Sell More Books with Less Social Media: Spend Less Time Marketing and More Time Writing (Chris Syme)
http://tinyurl.com/LessSocialMedia

Text Me! Snap Me! Ask Me Anything!: How Entrepreneurs, Consultants And Artists Can Use The Power of Intimate Attention To Build Their Brand, Grow Their Business And Change The World (Kevin Kruse)
http://tinyurl.com/TextMeSnapMe

The AdWeek Copywriting Handbook: The Ultimate Guide to Writing Powerful Advertising and Marketing Copy from One of America's Top Copywriters (Joseph Sugarman)
http://tinyurl.com/AdWeekCopy

Reader Magnets: Build Your Author Platform and Sell more Books on Kindle (Nick Stephenson)
http://tinyurl.com/ReaderMagnet

On Writing: A Memoir of the Craft (Stephen King)
http://tinyurl.com/SKingOnWriting

Your First 1000 Copies: The Step-by-Step Guide to Marketing Your Book (Tim Grahl)
http://tinyurl.com/First1000Copies

You Must Write a Book: Boost Your Brand, Get More Business, and Become the Go-To Expert (Honorée Corder)
http://tinyurl.com/YouMustWriteaBook

The Miracle Morning for Writers: How to Build a Writing Ritual That Increases Your Impact and Your Income (Hal Elrod & Steve Scott, with Honorée Corder)
http://tinyurl.com/MM4Writers

WRITING AND SELF-PUBLISHING PODCASTS TO LISTEN TO:

Authors' note: There are so many great podcasts, this is not the full list, just a few of our favorites to get you started.

The Author Biz Podcast
TheAuthorBiz.com

The Author Hangout
BookMarketingTools.com/blog

The Self-Publishing Podcast
SterlingandStone.net/podcasts

The Sell More Books Show
SellMoreBooksShow.com

The Smarty Pants Book Marketing Podcast
SmartyPantsBookMarketing.libsyn.com/podcast

The Wordslinger Podcast
KevinTumlinson.com/podcast-rss

The Writer Files Podcast
Rainmaker.fm

QUICK FAVOR

We're wondering, did you enjoy this book?

First of all, thank you for reading our book! May we ask a quick favor?

Will you take a moment to leave an honest review for this book on Amazon? Reviews are the BEST way to help others purchase the book.

You can go to the link below and write your thoughts. We appreciate you!

HonoreeCorder.com/FindingReadersReview

GRATITUDE

GENERAL THANKS

To my husband, partner, and best friend, Byron.

To my daughter and inspiration, Lexi, I'm so grateful to be your mom.

To my mastermind peeps, Rich, Andrea, and Brian - I'm so grateful for your support, ideas, and our synergy.

Who is Honorée

Honorée Corder is the author of dozens of books, including *You Must Write a Book, Prosperity for Writers* and *The Prosperous Writer* book series, *Vision to Reality*, *Business Dating*, *The Successful Single Mom* book series, *If Divorce is a Game, These are the Rules*, and *The Divorced Phoenix*. She is also Hal Elrod's business partner in *The Miracle Morning* book series. Honorée coaches business professionals, writers, and aspiring non-fiction authors who want to publish their books to bestseller status, create a platform, and develop multiple streams of income. She also does all sorts of other magical things, and her badassery is legendary. You can find out more at HonoreeCorder.com.

Honorée Enterprises, Inc.
Honoree@HonoreeCorder.com
http://www.HonoreeCorder.com
Twitter: @Honoree
& @Singlemombooks
Facebook: http://www.facebook.com/Honoree

Who is Brian

Brian D. Meeks (sometimes Arthur Byrne) is a full-time author who writes fiction under his name and the name of his protagonist from *Underwood, Scotch, and Wry*, Arthur Byrne. He has released 12 novels, with the 13th on the way. In addition to mysteries, thrillers, YA, science fiction, and satire, he writes non-fiction with his co-author Honorée Corder about the business of writing and publishing. He lives in Iowa, travels whenever he can, and follows lots of guinea pigs on Facebook because they are freaking adorable.

EcocandleRiel@gmail.com

The Prosperous Writer Book Series

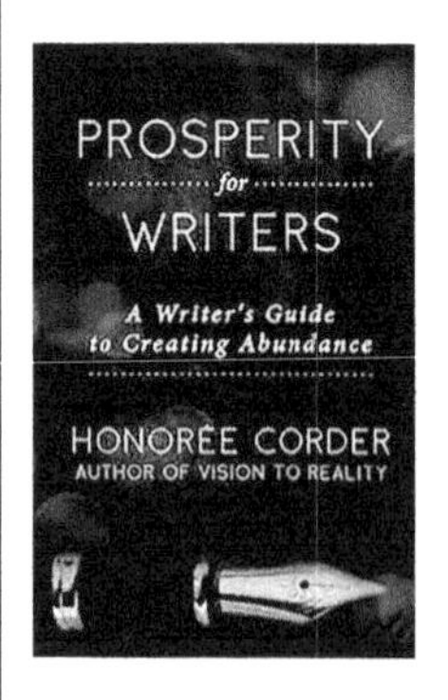

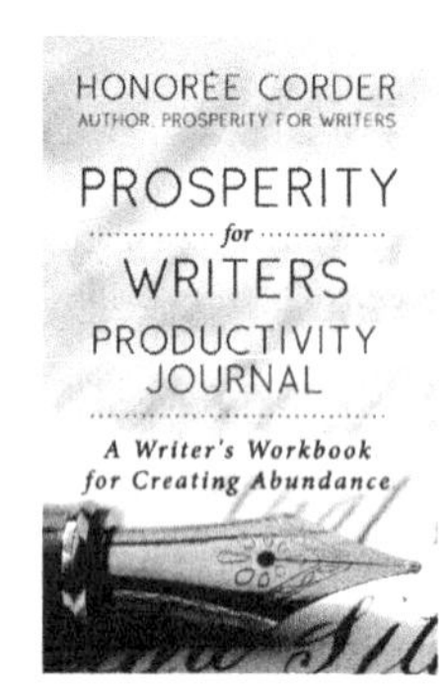

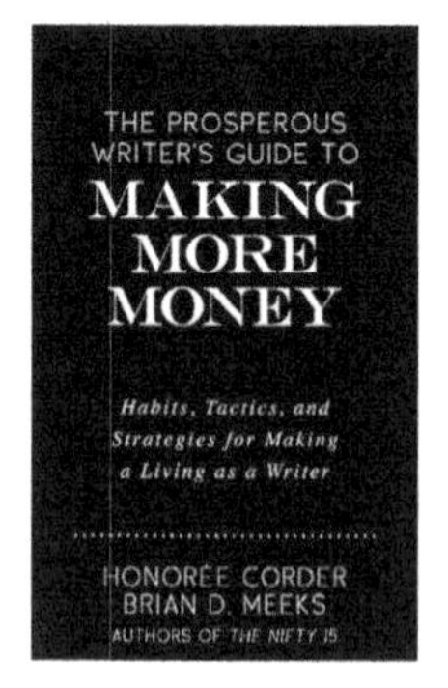

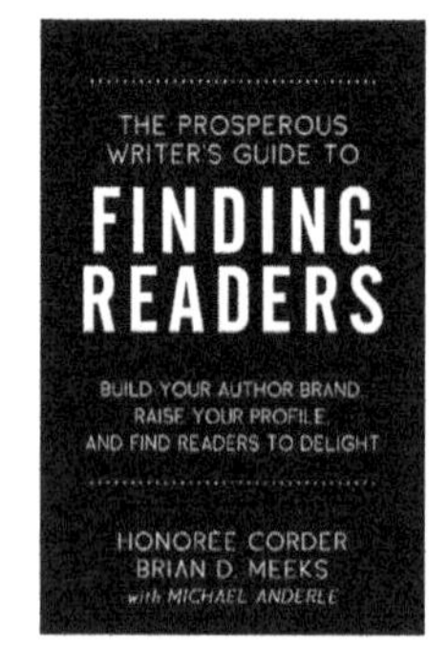

Coming Soon ...

The Prosperous Writer Mindset

Made in the USA
Las Vegas, NV
01 May 2021

22333931R10207